In Business And In Love

**How Couples Can
Successfully Run
A Marriage-Based
Business**

Chuck and Aprill Jones

In Business And In Love

Chuck and Aprill Jones

Copyright © 2003 by Chuck and Aprill Jones
ISBN 0-938716-59-X

Published by
Possibility Press

Manufactured in the United States of America

Special Recommendation
by Peggy Britt

———— ♥♥ ————

In Business *And* In Love

In Business And In Love is helpful reading, especially for young couples trying to organize their responsibilities at home, with their responsibilities to their business. There are tips on what works well for managing family, time, and money, while making personal time for each other on the life-long journey to success.

I think you will really enjoy this book. Your time reading it will be well spent!

Peggy Britt
Crown Ambassador

Acknowledgments

To our parents for the love and discipline in which we were raised, and the encouragement to develop our talents and gifts in a safe, secure environment.

To Cindy, Jason, and Ran, for all the fun times, laughs, and lessons of life. And to all our friends who have been our cheerleaders, sources of encouragement, and best-buddies.

Aprill: To my English teachers at Warren County Senior High, particularly Douglas Reed and Elizabeth Womack. You saw in me a gift, and your recognition of that has been a source of inspiration my entire life.

Chuck: To Professor Richard Joel who helped set my career in the direction it is still going to this day. And to Dr. Donald Hileman who encouraged me to "go far, do much, and never be afraid of adventure."

Dedication

To God, our Father, who has blessed our life together
in ways we never imagined.

And to you, our readers. We sincerely hope your lives
will be enriched by what we have shared.

Table of Contents

Introduction—Our Dream Came True 6

1. What If This Is As Good As It Gets? 8

2. Countering the "Why Nots" 15

3. It Was the Best of Times and...
   The Most Challenging of Times! 25

4. Who's On First? 36

5. Money Matters 47

6. It's 7 a.m. Already—Why Aren't You Up? 64

7. Did You Turn the Copier Off? 72

8. You're Doing *What?* 79

9. Sorry, Honey—I've Grown Very Fond of Eating .. 90

10. Little Karen's Quite a Salesperson! 100

11. Home Sweet Office, Office Sweet Home 115

12. The Payoffs of Working Together 127

13. The Exciting Journey...Home 130

About the Authors 144

Introduction

———❤———

Our Dream Came True!

After All, We Got Married To Be Together

When we first got the idea of writing a book about how a husband and wife team can start, build, and successfully operate a business together, we asked each other this question:

How can our experiences help other couples?

We reflected on the past and considered the following:

❤ We've been married seventeen years, and this is the one and only marriage for both of us.

❤ We enjoy a full and total commitment to each other, and hold that commitment sacred—not to be compromised at any time, in any way, for any purpose.

❤ We have a strong desire that our relationship be more comprehensive and engaging than any other relationship we have. We had always wanted more than the *6 p.m. to 10 p.m. weekdays and between errands on weekends* relationships that average working couples have.

♥ Finally, and above all others, we have a strong faith in God, and believe in the institution of marriage as the best way for us to live.

In short, we are happily married. We have always been happy to be married to each other. However, we believe the *greater* level of happiness we now enjoy is a direct result of deciding to start, build, sustain, and nurture our own marriage-based business! After all, we got married to be together. And running a marriage-based business is the only way we know of doing this to the max.

Along the way, we've learned a thing or two, had a lot of successes, and some failures, too. After stepping back and looking at them all, we decided that there were some nuggets of information that would probably apply to any couple considering working together as a husband-and-wife team.

So here it is. We hope you find it helpful. And when you do decide to build your own business, or perhaps become more active with your spouse in the one you already have, we hope you will achieve much success and happiness. As you grow your business together, you'll develop a closeness to each other that couples who don't operate a business together will never understand or realize.

May your dream come true as it has for us. Go for it. You'll be glad you did.

Enjoy!

Chuck and April Jones

Chapter 1

———— ❥ ————

What If This Is As Good As It Gets?

Your Marriage Could Be Happier Than Ever

Is Your Marriage What You Thought It Would Be?

Sooner or later, if you haven't already, you and your spouse are likely going to wake up one morning, look at each other and ask: *"When we got married, did you think it was going to be like this?"*

Or, as an actor in a hit movie once put it, *"What if this is as good as it gets?"*

But, unfortunately, that's not the worst of it. Today, most families are two-income—meaning there are *two* people in the same situation. That's double-trouble! Many couples spend the time they aren't at work shuttling children to and from band practice, soccer games, or other activities. Or perhaps they impose on friends and relatives to do so. They prepare and eat quick dinners or grab non-nutritious fast food from the nearest corner outlet.

Once home, they rush from homework to lawn work, from washing the clothes to bathing the children, from making lunches to making three dozen cupcakes for a Girl Scout meeting, and from cleaning the house to cleaning the garage. You can make your own list.

And at the end of each chaotic day, they collapse in bed— too tired to be intimate, too tired to read, and many times too tired to even talk. Their reward? They get to do it all over again tomorrow. It's a fairly common occurrence. And why wouldn't it be? Think about it for a moment:

The average person who works for the typical corporation spends between 45 and 60 hours each week working. Factoring in a liberal three to four weeks of vacation (which most people do not get), that translates into three to four continuous months of work for every week off—at best!

Now, during that same 48-week period, if the same person spends 6 hours each weekday and 16 hours each weekend day with his or her spouse and children, that person will enjoy 4 continuous months of family time for every 11. But that means 6 hours *every* weekday, and 16 hours *every* day of *every* weekend. So at the *very best*, the average person works as much or more time than they spend with their spouse and family.

For Better or Worse, in Presence or Absence?

That's not the way most of us had it planned when we said our *I dos*. Our vision of marriage may not have been the Cleavers, (an "ideal family" portrayed on the '60s U.S. sitcom, *Leave It To Beaver*), but it wasn't the Jetsons (a '60s TV cartoon show with a space age futuristic slant) either. We wanted something pretty simple: for our lives to get better, and for us to be together.

The tragedy is this—the average husband and wife spend most of their time apart from each other as well as their children! We know, because we used to be an average couple.

But six years ago, we got tired of being average! For Chuck, there was a single moment that defined his search for a new direction. Some might say it was a flash of brilliance, while others may call it a mark of stupidity. We know what it really was—*a glaring realization of the obvious.*

Chuck

It happened one evening while driving home from yet another long day at the office. Who knows why, but I started doing a short life assessment:

- ♥ I am 30 years old.
- ♥ I have a beautiful and charming wife whom I love with all my heart.
- ♥ I have a nice home in a wonderful warm-weather climate.
- ♥ I have a really funny basset hound named Elmo who is always ready to play.
- ♥ I live two hours from the southern Appalachian Mountains, and three hours from the Atlantic coast.
- ♥ I have four guitars and a piano.
- ♥ I belong to an active church involved in more good works than I can list.
- ♥ And, I have virtually no time to enjoy any of them.

I was home before I knew it—one of those frightening driving experiences when you don't remember any of the usual landmarks, none of the instances of the particular trip. You just suddenly arrive without remembering anything. That's how hard I was thinking about the state of my life.

April and I would soon celebrate our 9th wedding anniversary, and it had become common for us to spend only one or two hours a day together. And those were the leftover hours—the ones with a lot of yawning, sighing, and glassy-eyed stares. It was about all I had left after 14- to 16-hour days. And some weeks were worse with two to three nights of overnight travel.

Because Aprill's job was more 8:30 to 5:30, she had hours and hours alone. Most days she woke up after I had already left for work, and she got home first every day. Dinnertime was never a constant. Trying to predict when I would arrive home was impossible. Some nights it was 7 p.m., others 9. Sometimes I would call at 7 and say I was on my way, only to be snagged at the office door for an impromptu one- hour discussion. Late again.

But for Aprill, her biggest frustration was that she had lost control of her day-to-day life.

Aprill

I found myself in a fairly good job situation. It wasn't perfect. But, nonetheless, it was good enough to motivate me to get up every morning, put on those pantyhose, squeeze my feet into those pumps, endure lower back pain from the commute, and smile on payday.

But things could have been better—*a lot better*. It would have been nice to have more flexible hours, the freedom to make my own schedule. Then I could go grocery shopping at some time other than Saturday—when the store was packed with others like me, who were momentarily out of their "cage."

Even though my boss was a very nice man, I still did not want him in charge of so much of my life. But he was. When I agreed to take the job, I gave up control of the hours of my day when I was most energetic and productive. All I had left for Chuck or myself, for that matter, was the remnants of spent energy.

And as the pace seemed to get more and more chaotic, I couldn't help but feel there surely must be more to life than working and saving for retirement.

I found myself envious at times of my stay-at-home mom friends, until I realized it wasn't a lot better for them. They didn't have a perfect situation either. But from my point of view, at least they did get to wear sneakers every day of the week and they didn't have to pay for day care.

Of course, many complained that they virtually never got to interact with adults, never had a reason to stop eating between meals, and never had any extra money. But how would they ever find a job situation that would allow them to build a schedule around "Mother's Mornings Out" and pediatrician appointments? The pull of *the real world* was strong for these moms, and several of my friends didn't know how much longer they could wait for that *perfect* situation.

Regardless, I had come to agree with Chuck. *This wasn't how it was supposed to be.*

We married for better or worse, richer or poorer, in sickness and in health. We didn't marry for present or absent. In essence, we married to spend our lives together, not to be in separate, divergent pursuits of individual careers.

Don't misunderstand—we had nine enjoyable years of marriage behind us. We were well-traveled and had bonded with some common interests. We laughed a lot, had a good network of friends, and liked our positions as *up-and-comers* in our respective companies. The future was bright. Still, something was definitely wrong. We were wasting our lives by spending too much time being away from our best friend—each other.

After time alone with our thoughts, a pivotal moment came. Chuck hadn't told me about his revelation during his drive home that one evening. And I hadn't told him about my frustrations either. This was about to change though. As I walked by the sofa one night and casually said, "Listen to this—no one on his deathbed ever says 'I wish I had spent more time at the office!'"

The Start of Something Big

Kaboom! That simple statement did it. From that point on, our priorities shifted immediately and dramatically. We decided it was important and about time to fulfill our marriage vows as we had originally intended them.

We wanted to spend our lives *with* each other. And this was key—*we wanted it badly enough to overcome our fears of giving up regular paychecks.* Others call it job security. We now call it the myth of the paycheck. (More on that in Chapter 2.)

We had the *what* covered. We even had the *why* covered. Now we had to figure out the *how*....

We weren't wealthy. We weren't even well-off. We weren't even well. We had a mortgage, two car payments, credit card bills and all the other symbols of middle-class American success. Quitting work and retiring at 30 was totally out of the question. We had to work, so why not *together*? And in the politically correct 1990s, where spouses working for the same company was frowned upon, that most likely meant starting and building our own business. It wasn't just a major shift for us—it was a total social and economic overhaul for our family unit.

Eight years later, we are certain of one thing—it was the best decision we ever made. We now spend our mornings, afternoons, and evenings together. And we have several hours every day to pursue our own individual interests, without the guilt of always being apart!

Jokingly, we tell our friends that there are three types of married people: First, there are those who don't work with their spouses and don't want to try. Second are those who work with their spouses and love it. And third are those who realize that they've lost a lot of control in their lives. Yet, they just wonder if they could work with their spouses, but never take the necessary action to make it happen. That leads us to a hidden truth:

Group three is full of people who could happily be in group two! They have the desire, the skills and the temperament to pull it off. And, they have the most important reason of all—the need to regain more control of their lives, especially the time they can spend with their spouses and children.

Which group are you in? Here's an exercise that may help you find out:

To how many of the following questions would you answer *yes*?

- ♥ Do you love your spouse?
- ♥ Do you ever wish your lifestyle was one that allowed you to spend more time with your spouse and children?
- ♥ Do your children's activities and life requirements (like meals, preparation for school, and extracurricular activities) take more than 25 percent of your leisure time?
- ♥ Do you ever find yourself thinking that life would be easier if you had more control over the necessities of living (such as going to the grocery store, cutting the lawn, and getting the car serviced)?
- ♥ Do you go to sleep every night with something you consider important still left undone?
- ♥ Do you frequently give up your daily quiet time (or what could be that) for things that you feel forced to declare more urgent?

Here's the surprise: If you answered yes to even *one* of the questions, you are a prime candidate for a happier life working with your spouse. But don't just take our word for it...read on!

Chapter 2

---❦---

Countering the "Why Nots"

Most Couples Can Work Together

To Work Together or Not to Work Together

For every ten reasons to decide to work with your spouse, there's one reason why not to.

At first that statement is likely to sound a little strange to you—because it's totally opposite from what society would have you believe. (Friends and family may give you ten *why nots* for every *why* you come up with!)

One thing's for sure—when you announce to your friends and family that you and your husband have decided to build your own business, or that you've decided to quit your job and work with your spouse in the business he or she has built, the critics will come out of the woodwork. It seems that everyone east of the Mississippi has a reason *why not*. Most are entirely unsolicited. And, ironically, you'll discover that the most passionate naysayers have *never even tried* working with their spouse. To put it politely, they are absolutely unqualified to even make a statement on the topic.

In our case, that didn't stop them. It didn't even slow them down.

Aprill

The thought of working together never scared us. We have been blessed with a relationship made to last a lifetime. In fact, our story sounded like something from an old Sandra Dee movie:

> We met each other in junior high school and became high-school sweethearts a year later. We followed that with college. By the time Chuck graduated from college, we had been a couple for six years. We married a year later and moved from Tennessee to a "foreign land"—upstate New York—just to experience another part of the country.

By the time Chuck had his revelation on the drive home, and I began to question the control I had (or didn't have) in my career, we'd been together for almost fifteen years!

Before we ever considered working together, we had already passed every "good-marriage test" up to that point. We could cook an entire meal together...in the same kitchen. Chuck taught me how to drive a standard transmission car the day after we were married (and *that* was no honeymoon!). We built a house together. We had spent the first three years of our marriage one thousand miles from our nearest relatives. And we had lived to laugh about all of it.

Going Against the Odds

So, you can probably imagine our surprise when we began hearing things like:

"Are you crazy? You can't work with your wife."

"I could never work with my husband. We'd kill each other."

"Won't you get tired of being together?"

"I need my space. If I worked with my wife, I'd feel smothered."

"You're a brave man."

And our personal favorite:

"But, you all have such a great marriage. Why risk ruining it?"

Tired of being together? Feel smothered? Brave man?
Risk ruining a great marriage?
What was going on? For every note of encouragement we received, we heard ten *why nots*. What was most surprising to us was our own reactions to the *why nots*. They didn't dampen our enthusiasm for wanting to work with each other. Instead, we felt badly for all of these naysayers, who didn't want to work with their own spouses. (Do you think they, deep down inside, may have been envious of us?)

It's difficult to talk about how you love your spouse and how you look forward to spending every day with him or her when you see doubt, amusement, and "Oh, you are so young and naive," in their eyes. It's hard to hear so much discouragement over an issue you had not even considered—"Could you stand each other enough to be with each other all day every day?"

We knew that we could talk to friends who were already happily working together, if we needed advice and encouragement. We were friends with a couple who ran a full-service gas station together, another who had a mailing fulfillment company, a third who had their own independent network marketing business, and also a couple who owned and operated an insurance agency.

When we shared our experiences with the reactions of family and friends, they mostly just nodded their heads and smiled. We could see quickly that they liked what they were doing and working together, but they also knew we would have to find our own way—that each couple's experiences are similar in some ways, and different in others.

We decided the best way to prove it to ourselves, our families, and everyone else was—*to just do it*. And to succeed. Our resolve strengthened, and we began to transform the idea into action.

We have always risen to the occasion when we were told we couldn't do something we *knew* we *could* do. The only thing we knew we couldn't do was out-talk the naysayers.

After all, how can you tell someone that, if they feel that way, maybe they *couldn't* work together? (At least until they changed their attitude, that is!)

The Three Types of Why Nots

As we put together our ideas, the almost constant barrage of negatives never stopped. We found that *why nots* generally fall into one of three categories. And when you understand the nature of the *why not*, and you have the desire to overcome it, you're then better able to freely counter it with logic and positive action.

Why Not #1—Individual Concern: *"I'll Lose My Identity" and "I Won't Have Any Time to Myself."*

Many people are afraid to live life without a *label*. This notion may be completely foreign to them. Careers provide many of those labels—Insurance Agent, Creative Director, Plumber, Office Manager, Teacher, Engineer, Stockbroker, and the list goes on.

In some situations, to give up your *label* and work with your spouse may seem like you're losing your identity. This is understandable. As insane as this may sound, many people actually *need* their titles more than they need their positions! They latch onto them much like a child does with its security blanket. It's almost as if they feel they are nothing without a label—that they're not intrinsically valuable as a human being.

Think about it for a minute. When was the last time you met someone at a social function who didn't ask *what do you do* within the first two questions?

Tragically, for many of us, we believe that *what we do* is *who we are*. We have lost our sense of self and gotten it entangled in our roles. We may be so busy molding ourselves to carry out our roles, that we lose touch with who we are and what we stand for.

So, to many people caught in this quandary, the prospect of working with their spouse means they become, well, just *married*. They've fallen out of their previous role identity.

How do *you* answer the question, *"What do you do"?*

Others are actually concerned that, giving up their time away from home—away from their spouse and children—will somehow deprive them of their personal time. To them work is an escape. This is so, even though the act of working and the mechanics of living as a member of the working-class are often devastating. In fact, surveys show that seventy percent of working people dislike, or even hate, going to work. So the grind of being on the work "merry-go-round" is a physically and mentally taxing experience that seems to get worse every day.

Yet, despite all the challenges inherent in the job scene, in some strange way, they believe getting out of the house, away from their family and spouse, is the only way to keep their individuality, and their sanity! And as crazy and un-nurturing (to say the least) as most work environments are, they still provide *a way out*.

The vast majority of people don't realize that their perception of themselves and their roles need to shift 180° in the other direction! What you do could best *enable* you to be who you are, but it's grossly inappropriate that it *dictate* who you are in any way, shape or form. Once again, if people give their jobs that much importance in their lives, they relinquish a major portion of the precious control they need in order to be fully functioning, happy, and fulfilled.

It seems as though your family would be the last thing you'd want to abandon for the so-called freedom of going to work. It goes against the natural order of things. Since prehistoric times, mankind has relied on the family to provide a safe haven where its members can be most peaceful, comfortable, and who they really are—where they can discover their true identity.

When you change your focus from running away *from* your family to running *to* it, the prospect of greater personal development comes into focus. And it can lead to ultimate happiness and success. As you grow, you can structure your life so you build time for yourself. You don't need to get out of the house and into the "rat race" to accomplish that.

Why Not #2—Relationship Concern: *"Being Married and Working Together Are Two Different Things."*
More than once, we've heard comments like these:

> You have a good, strong marriage. You obviously love to be together. You share the same interests and the same values. And your strengths compliment each other. But working together is a whole different thing. What are you going to do when you have a difference of opinion? What if one of you wants to do one thing and the other wants something entirely different? What if...what if...?

Of all the *why nots* we've heard, this group represents the most ridiculous. Chuck quickly put his response into a single statement:

> If you get along around the breakfast table, you can probably get along around the conference table. If you don't get along well at breakfast, then you probably don't get along well at dinner, at your children's baseball games, at work in the yard, or anywhere else. This probably means you won't be able to get along working together. In fact, your marriage may need some help.

This realization can be one of the best things that could happen. It can cause you to slow down a little and take notice of some marital issues you may have been avoiding. And, while this may be a little more complex than what you expected, that's okay—you're certainly not alone.

Many people can't imagine working with their spouse because their relationship isn't strong enough to withstand another variable, particularly one as important as the livelihood of the family. But, the sad truth could be this: Their relationship has probably weakened because they haven't invested enough time in nurturing it. Remember when you were dating each other? Didn't you spend a *lot* of time together? Well, here's the hidden truth:

Quality relationships require time.

Now you may be thinking, "Well, Bob and Debbie have a great relationship. And he travels four days a week. She works second shift, and they hardly ever see each other—except on weekends!"

More power to Bob and Debbie. They may have a strong relationship or it may just *appear* that way. They may simply want to give that impression because they're afraid to face the truth. Or they may be like the occasional report of the 85-year-old man who smoked three packs of cigarettes a day for 60 years. He had no sign of lung cancer at all, but died by slipping and falling into the Grand Canyon on his 25th hike to the bottom!

The point is, most marriages are weak, as reflected partially by today's high divorce rate. And just because people stay married for years, and even decades, does not mean they have an excellent (or even good) marriage. Why? Because they don't devote enough time to their marriage to make it strong. They're sort of on "automatic," with their lives based on habits and routines. The often-beleaguered marriage gets whatever time is left over. And the children get the time just before whatever is left over.

Think about it—would you want your doctor to perform your surgery during the middle of the morning, or at 10 p.m.—after he's already performed eleven?

Why Not #3—Financial Concern: *"You Shouldn't Put All Your Eggs In One Basket."*

Finally, we realized perhaps the most important point of all. Virtually everyone who has spent his or her entire life so far working for someone else falls victim to *the myth of the paycheck.* It's quite simple to explain.

For most of us (and we count ourselves as former members of the *most*), the weekly, bi-weekly or monthly paycheck is our visual symbol of stability. We do our jobs and, for that effort, we receive compensation—which usually doesn't represent what we are worth. It's simply the compensation we receive for the job we do. We're typically paid only what the job is worth, not what we're worth!

The paycheck(s) becomes the core of our financial plan and the way we live our lives. We budget our monthly expenses around it. We draw from it to meet our obligations. And we rely on it to provide food and shelter, as well as support our leisure activities.

The paycheck is also the guardian of our children. With what's left over, we may send them to college or private school. It provides their clothes, supplies and the gas for the minivan or sport utility vehicle to motor them around from one practice to another.

Finally, if we carve it up wisely, it may even be large enough to protect *us* in our later years.

Hopefully, we'll get to use it to build a nest egg to provide for our needs after we stop working.

The paycheck is, in a word, often perceived to be our *security.* And therein lies the myth. At the risk of sounding too dramatic, *this is one of the most potentially destructive myths we ever encounter.*

In order for something to truly represent security, it must genuinely be secure. And, for something to be secure, it must be in the control of the person for whom the security is important. This is the "Catch-22."

Even if you don't get anything else from this book, get this:

If you are working for someone else, you have *no* control over your paycheck. And if your paycheck represents your security, you have *no* control over your security. All your eggs are already in one basket—and someone else is holding it!

In today's society, nobody wants to be told which doctor to go to and parents want to choose which school they'd like their child to attend. No family wants a landfill put near *its* subdivision. In other words, virtually everyone wants control over their own lives. So tell us this: why then do so many people allow someone else to control their paychecks?

The Good Old Days

The answer is, who knows! But it wasn't always this way.

In our parents' and grandparents' generation, you could count on working for a company for 40 or 50 years. They would gladly keep you—and you would stay. And the person next to you would probably be there for 40 or 50 years too. You worked, got a regular paycheck, went home at the same time every day, and enjoyed job security.

But that was probably a totally foreign idea for one person in your family—your great-grandfather. He probably worked for himself. He made his own decisions. He likely owned a farm and his wife handled an equal share of the responsibilities. Or, perhaps they ran a general store together...or a livery stable...or some other family-owned and -operated business.

They enjoyed control over *their* paycheck. If business was down, they made the necessary decisions to turn it around. If one crop failed, they planted another. If there was a drought, they irrigated the fields.

In short, they worked together. What a revolutionary idea!

More importantly, they also enjoyed control over their *lives*. They answered to no one but the customer. They shared common goals in life—personal, professional, spiritual, and leisure. Children worked alongside their parents. No one relied on schools, daycare workers or neighbors to train their children; they did it themselves. Why? Because they had the time to do it. They didn't *make* the time—they *controlled* the time. Their time was truly *their* time!

Want to know how many marriages were first and only marriages? Most.

Want to know how many children the average family had? Four to six.

Want to know how high the divorce rate was? Almost non-existent.

Want to know how much time fathers, mothers, and children spent together? Outside of school, almost every waking hour.

Want to know why we so often refer to them as the good old days?

Decide for yourself....

Chapter 3

———— 🖤 ————

It Was the Best of Times and...the Most Challenging of Times!

The First 90 Days

Everything Has a Beginning...

Do you remember your first three months of first grade? How about your first three months of college? Or the first three months you were married?

Do you remember the first three months you were employed full-time? Or the first three months you owned your first home?

The first three months of any endeavor can be exciting and invigorating as well as challenging—all at the same time! And when faced with change, our bodies and minds respond. Some people choose to love change, and warmly embrace it, while others decide to dislike change and coldly resist it. So who do you suppose is happier in the long-run?

How *you* react to change is unique to *you*. And it's a decision only *you* can make. Decide to consider change an adventure and look for the good in it—you'll be glad you did!

The first three months of working with your spouse in your own business are likely to bring some exciting and profound changes to your relationship, which could affect many aspects of your life in a positive way. But, of course, it's impossible to know how you will respond and grow during your first three months of working together. So perhaps our stories about our first three months in business together will give you some ideas.

The First 90 Days According to Chuck

To understand how Aprill and I responded to working together during our first 90 days, you first need to read a story you may find difficult to believe!

I taught Aprill how to drive a manual transmission in a rented truck the day after we were married. We loaded everything she owned into it (I had moved six months earlier), and drove 1,000 miles to our new home. We felt sure we were in the Arctic tundra because it was so cold, but it was actually Schenectady, New York!

Now you may have never taken on the task of teaching someone how to operate a manual transmission car or truck, let alone your spouse. If not, you probably have no idea what an "amazing" experience you could be missing! I became convinced that day that regardless of what statistics tell you about troubled marriages and financial difficulties, teaching your spouse how to use the clutch...*Let it up easy. EASY! Now give it a little gas. No, not that much. WAIT!!! Okay, that was good. Now, let's try it again...* causes more disputes than any other single thing.

But our story didn't begin in a rented truck. It began much earlier...

We had a rather long history before we ever stepped into the truck. We started dating when we were still in high school and went to college together. So when we finally got into that truck, we had already dated for six years before we got married! We both pretty much knew what to expect when we started the driving lesson:

Like many people, Aprill would probably have lots of challenges learning how to drive a "stick." She may buck and stall it many times. We anticipated she may be frustrated enough to cry or, at least, confess that she didn't believe she would ever be able to learn to do it. All the while, though, we knew she would engage her typical bulldog tenacity to succeed. Her unyielding perseverance would undoubtedly—much sooner than she ever anticipated—result in her achieving exceptional success in clutching, shifting and driving the truck.

It would be easy for me to be understanding, supportive and empathetic, at least in the beginning. I would explain the process, and possibly demonstrate my "expertise" (even though I had never owned a vehicle with manual transmission, and probably had fewer than four hours total behind the wheel of any car or truck that wasn't an automatic!).

Then, as Aprill "got her feet wet" (began her learning curve), I would probably become increasingly frustrated. I'd have to be careful that her frustration wouldn't fuel my frustration until, finally, I might profess, too, that I didn't believe she would ever be able to do it. I'd need to work to maintain my positive, encouraging state of mind to continue to be genuinely understanding, supportive and empathetic. And when she would start clutching and shifting with ease, I would congratulate her repeatedly and suggest we celebrate over pizza.

Interestingly enough, it did turn out similarly to what we expected—pizza and all! How come?

A big part of making the first three months of working together a successful launching pad is in anticipating what to expect, based on what you already know about your spouse. You need to expect the positive as much as possible while, at the same time, understanding your spouse's tendencies and preferences so you can be more supportive.

Aprill is what has become fashionably known as *left-brained*. She strongly values order. She loves to learn by the book, preferably in a classroom setting. She will read an instruction manual from cover to cover and devour computer tutorials. She is quite a reader. She can read four books in the time it takes me to read one. Aprill is also an adept budgeter.

At the same time, she has an adventurous side about her that is definitely not left-brained. But it isn't right-brained either. So we call it her no-brained side. For instance, she looks at a recipe for a 15-ingredient gourmet dish she's never cooked. She then makes some major modifications of her own, prepares it, and serves it as the main course to six new friends whom we've never had to our home before. Her first taste is everyone else's first taste as well. A brave soul indeed! (And, remarkably, the food always tastes terrific too.)

I, on the other hand, am what I call *a right-brained, left-brained wanna-be*. I rarely make to-do lists, even though I know they would help me immeasurably. I love order, but even though I'm far from being a slob, I rarely have things as orderly as I would like them. I neatly fold my socks, t-shirts, underwear and other clothes in a way that only I can do to my satisfaction. I meticulously sort them all and have a place for everything. Then, when I take my clothes off at the end of the day, I throw everything into the bottom of my closet making piles that I clear only when they get so high I can't function!

Unlike Aprill, I detest owners manuals, how-to instructions and tutorials. I prefer to learn by trial and error. I'm a musician. I play guitar, piano, and even a little mandolin. I can read music, but never do because I'd rather play it the way *I* want to play it—not the way someone else has played it before.

At the same time, I'll study specs and look at ten, twenty or thirty models—many two, three or four times each—before I'll purchase an inexpensive clock radio!

I knew those things about Aprill, and she knew those things about me. After all, by the time we started working together, we had been together (dating and married) for 16 years! Still, that didn't mean our first three months were an easy "walk in the park."

In our case, I started the business and had been building it for two years before Aprill joined me. (This may be somewhat unusual. Oftentimes, couples begin their new business venture together on a part-time basis as they both work their day jobs, and this is generally recommended as a financially safer alternative. But we'll talk more about that later.)

I was doing things in my own semi-chaotic, to the casual observer, way. My desk was messy, but my financial books were immaculate. My filing system was almost nonexistent, but I could still give you an update on everything I was doing. And I had learned all the computer software programs needed to run the business. But, I couldn't teach Aprill any of them because I didn't have a clue as to how I had learned them!

Aprill took one look at how things were going and she jumped right in, and did her level best to work in my style. She worked a lot harder to adjust to me than I did to adjust to her. It wasn't malice on my part, just ignorance. The business was gaining momentum, and I assumed she would *get with the program*. But even knowing her as well as I did, I forgot one thing. She is not "wired" as I am. I knew that; I had just forgotten about it.

I learned along the way that you simply can't anticipate everything your spouse will say or do, regardless of how well you know them. So another big part of making the first three months successful is understanding that your differences are far from being a negative. The truth is, differences are not only good—they're great! They eliminate boredom and help you balance each other out. Appreciate them.

I was pretty good at keeping records, and an adequate money manager. April, on the other hand, is a meticulous bookkeeper, and an outstanding money manager. Her propensity to budget, analyze expenses, anticipate revenues and plan accordingly far exceeds my abilities and interests in those aspects. Her adventurous side makes her superb at creative conceptualization. And since concepts are the lifeblood of any advertising and graphic design agency, that's a good thing. Her love of reading has also given her a vocabulary and an ability to write that has expanded the capabilities of our business and enhanced the value we can offer our clients.

While Aprill has a bold streak, she is somewhat averse to taking risks. I, on the other hand, am much more comfortable with risk. So, I am more willing to expand with new capabilities and service offerings. Because of her tendency to budget, she is more apt to want to know the exact return on anything we invest in. That, in turn, has made her an even better money manager by increasing her knowledge of financing and capital management. It has also given her satisfaction by offering her more avenues for her creative talents, like writing this book!

Yes! The first 90 days can be an adventurous challenge. And, how you approach them will determine, in large measure, how quickly you succeed. Your attitude and responses to the challenges, as you work through them as a team, can take you to a brand new, exciting level of understanding and love for each other—like nothing else can! Know that you can have a rocky first three months and still succeed, even though it may slow you down some. Invite and celebrate change. As you adapt to your new working relationship, do your best to be prepared and flexible. Understand each other's traits well because you'll need them, like all businesspeople do, as you grow yourselves and your business.

The First 90 Days According to Aprill

The happy day did finally arrive. I was about to join a new business and have a new lifestyle. I felt really ready for it and full of mixed emotions—both happiness and trepidation! On my last day of the job, which finally came in mid-November, my co-workers threw a little party for me. Chuck, who was already on that wonderful flexible schedule, also came, and everyone seemed genuinely happy for me. Can you picture *your* early retirement party?

My first entrepreneurial adventure was to help prepare for and assist in a photo shoot. The days before the shoot were filled with errands—picking up various items for the shoot. And since we were going to do the shoot at our house, I spruced up the area so it would be ready for the camera.

We had a lot of fun doing the shoot on a beautiful fall day. We started early in the morning in a park and ended late in the day at home. Along with our client and the photographer, we ate pizza in our garage on our lunch break and got our own dogs in the shoot. It was a fantastic day and a great start. I was going to love this business, I could just tell.

Then it came time for me to learn the Macintosh computer, so I used the instruction manuals as my guides. I started playing around on America Online, hoping that just by fingering the keyboard I would somehow learn to run MYOB (business accounting software), Microsoft Word, and Quark through osmosis. "Just start messing around with it. That's how I learned it," Chuck told me. I discovered, gratefully, I didn't need to be a computer whiz to make a go of this.

At first, though, I must admit that I felt like an idiot. Realistically, I could follow the tutoring programs or the manuals' "Let's Get Started" sections, but I didn't really like learning that way. I wanted Chuck, a warm, real human, to teach me. But that wasn't going to happen. Chuck didn't have the time nor the inclination to be my personal computer tutor. He was doing his best just to keep our business going—which was more important than ever since I had quit my job.

I adopted the morning routine of getting up, getting dressed and getting out of the house. I checked our post office box and picked up any mail, filed, delivered proofs, and listened to and observed what Chuck was doing as I continued learning more about the business. In the afternoon, I generally invested some time with the computer and my manuals. I remained ecstatic with my newly found freedom. I had no boss and no set hours—yea!

But when the winter weather set in with cold and rain, and I thought I had basically found my new rhythm, something happened to me. I "crashed."

Christmas was fast approaching—a season that normally meant a ridiculous amount of time spent socializing, entertaining, shopping, cooking, and such. But I really didn't want to get involved with all that. My mood remained good. I still got up, got dressed, and put on makeup every morning, but I didn't want to see or talk to anyone but Chuck.

I got through the season pretty much in that mode. I didn't go backward, if you will, but I didn't do much to go forward in my new career/business role, either. Chuck was very understanding and did not push or prod. He just accepted all I had to give. On New Year's Eve I came down with a cold that lasted a week. After about my fifth day on the sofa, I looked at Chuck one evening and said, "Well, I guess I better get up and get to it tomorrow." "Yep," he responded. And I did. I was ready to go and go hard.

So, what had happened to me? It was basically the same thing that happened to Chuck when he, too, left the corporate battlefields. Letting all those battles and skirmishes go, feeling the relief that you don't have to face those things that brought you so much stress and pain before, just breathing that long, pure sigh of contentment can take it out of you. *It's like you finally got a life.* But, nonetheless, you may still need to recuperate and regroup from the days when you were in the grind.

Scientific studies I've read show that any life change, positive or seemingly negative (and believe me, self-employment with your spouse is positive), can cause some stress. So I retreated, as had Chuck, lived with all those emotions of the transition, got comfortable with my new life, then came out ready to take on the world.

We talked about our different learning styles. I was still having a hard time with the manuals, but Chuck wanted me to learn our business financial management program, MYOB, and take that portion of the business out of his hands. I had a negative attitude about learning this program and taking on the financial bookkeeping responsibilities. (You may be in a business that's simpler than ours, like being an independent business owner with a network of others, where a tried and true system of success is already in place. If so, consider yourself fortunate.) I expressed my disdain every day for about three months. But Chuck believed in me more than I believed in myself. He felt confident I would not plunge us headlong into ruin in the space of three months—or ever, for that matter.

During our first three months, I eventually signed up for desktop publishing courses at our community college. I enjoyed the classes and became more confident in my relationship with the Macintosh computer. This turned out to be a real benefit both for our business and our relationship! I was pulling my load, and it felt good.

Trust, a subject a lot of people like to talk about, was beginning to mean a lot more in our marriage. Having trust wasn't just knowing we were faithful, or that we wouldn't embarrass each other in front of other people. Trust meant demonstrating to one another the confidence we felt in each other's ability to make this business a success. What a revelation and a joy! And, what an opportunity to truly grow as individuals and as a couple!

As we went along, we noticed our work styles were different too, but not necessarily conflicting. I liked a neat, tidy desk with prioritized stacks, my favorite ballpoint pen, a highlighter, a felt tip pen, a desk calendar for quick reference, and my phone to the right. Chuck liked a scattered desk, a pencil, a portfolio schedule, and I'm not sure where he liked his phone, or if he even had a preference.

There's nothing wrong with either of our styles. But they *are* different. And that's all we needed to realize. Our attitude toward each other was this:

> You are you, no matter what you do or how you do it. You are the same person I married even though I didn't know about your business habits. And I love you even more because now I know things about you I didn't know before we became business partners!

Once we got over that easy hurdle, I wanted to tell everyone, "Take that, all you who thought it would ruin our marriage to work together!" Working together, as far as adjusting to your spouse's style, is not much different than learning to live in the same house or apartment. You can live in harmony and look the other way when something small or trivial bothers you, or you can make a big deal out of it—which is probably not a good idea.

You need to understand that your spouse may, at the very same moment you are upset about what he or she did, be experiencing a slight annoyance over something that *you* have or haven't done! You can choose to ignore it, or kindly state your preference, for example, "I would really appreciate it if you'd remember to turn off the computer." Or, you can give each other grief over the slightest infraction. It's your choice to make when you become husband and wife as well as business partners.

My guess would be that if you yell at each other in your personal life, that you will tend to do so while in business together too. I absolutely don't like yelling, and we've never done much of it in our life together. We didn't yell at each other during the first three months as business partners, and only maybe one other time in the last seven years over either a business or personal issue.

If the yelling doesn't bother you, and you want to work together anyway, just don't yell in front of your clients/customers or associates/employees. Also, refrain from yelling while on the phone, or over lunch. Just remember—how you handle personality issues in your marriage is sure to translate into your business communications with each other.

And there may be some personality issues. There may also be financial, home, and lifestyles issues. If you have children, you've got their personalities, needs, and wants incorporated into the whole mix. Lots, if not the majority of those issues, are likely to surface the first three months you are in business together—that is, if everyone is being open and honest in their communications.

Sometimes it's important to simply remember *why* you married and love your spouse. Other times, though, you are much better off *not* to be thinking of that. Instead, treat your spouse as you would another professional colleague or associate! You will spend the first six months to a year learning to know when to respond one way or the other. Be patient with yourselves and realize that this is a golden opportunity to grow both professionally and as a couple. Allow these experiences to bond you more closely to one another, as you work though the challenges and celebrate the victories.

Sometimes we *still* don't understand each other. I think Chuck is still a little puzzled that I like to take classes, and I still don't know how he can accomplish so much before 10 a.m.! But we don't care that we may not understand each other's style fully. The business is a success, and our marriage is stronger than ever. Our first three months as business partners helped us build the strong foundation we needed to make that happen.

Chapter 4

───❤───

Who's On First?

Each Spouse Needs to Have Certain Responsibilities

Imagine the Following Scene...

You and your spouse decide it's time to take the children on a long-overdue vacation. Perhaps it's to one of those areas in southern California or central Florida where there are lots of strange looking creatures with oversized heads and two-word names starting with the same letter. You have a weekend business convention to attend there, and have set aside a couple more days just to enjoy the area's attractions.

You arrive at the airport, park the car, and proceed to the ticketing area of a major airline. There are 235 people in line. Behind the counter checking tickets and tagging baggage are fifteen pilots. The procedure is a little different than any you've ever experienced before.

After the boarding passes are handed out, the pilots instruct the passengers to gather off to the side and wait. Once all 239 people are checked in (235 people originally in line, plus you, your spouse, and your two children), all fifteen pilots close the stations and walk the entire group to the plane. There they take your boarding passes, show you to your seats, close the doors, and all fifteen of them cram into the cockpit.

You look around and there isn't a flight attendant in sight. The plane is taxiing down the runway when, suddenly, it stops. The cockpit door flies open and all fifteen pilots spill out like circus clowns getting out of a small car. They proceed to show you and the other passengers how to fasten your safety belts, use the oxygen masks (in case they're needed) and to exit the plane in the unlikely event of an emergency. They then collect any cups, and request that you return your seat-back tray to its upright and locked position. After that, they all cram, once again, back into the cockpit—at which time the plane resumes its trip down the runway.

As odd as it seems, you shrug it off as the plane lifts off the end of the runway and climbs uneventfully to a cruising altitude of 35,000. Just then, the cabin speakers come alive with 15 voices saying in perfect unison, "Thank you for choosing Amazing Air Lines. In a moment, we'll be around the cabin to serve you complimentary beverages and a light snack." At almost that precise moment, the door of the cockpit flies open and all fifteen pilots pour out like some type of slow-moving liquid, and begin to serve beverages. And although you missed breakfast, you suddenly lose your appetite when your spouse looks at you and nervously asks, "Who's flying the plane, dear?"

Everyone Doesn't Get to Fly the Plane

On the surface, that's a pretty ridiculous tale. No airline would survive federal licensing, much less day-to-day operations, by running with such inefficiency and danger. In short, everyone who works at the airline doesn't fly the plane.

Sadly, many small businesses, especially those started by husband and wife teams, endeavor to do just that. Everyone does everything. Everyone is responsible for every task while no one is individually responsible for any particular task. No one is accountable because everyone is accountable. Some things get done twice while other things don't get done at all!

The same questions get answered to customers, prospects and associates/employees in two different ways—and both are right based on the perspective and knowledge of the person answering.

There are certainly exceptions, but here is another hidden truth to consider:

> Virtually all successful companies are made up of two or more individuals doing different but parallel functions to the same end—to produce a quality product or deliver a marketable service.

Can you imagine watching the production of a car if one person unloaded the raw materials, smelted and formed the metal, fabricated the plastic, then walked along the conveyor system and attached each and every piece until the car was complete? That used to be the way cars were made—before a man named Henry Ford came along and created the assembly line. Because at that, it is highly unlikely that anyone reading this book drives a car completely and totally constructed by hand, especially with the high-tech equipment now on those assembly lines!

On a side note, can you name any brands of cars that were successful before the Ford Model-T? Didn't think so.

You Take Care of This, and I'll Handle That

One of the critical factors in the long-term success of your new business is an early sharing of responsibilities between you and your spouse. This is best done by considering what you each enjoy and do best as the deciding factor of who'll do what. Then honor those arrangements even if your spouse performs his or her role differently than you would do it.

This accomplishes several things:

First, it assures that necessary tasks will be done because there is always someone accountable. For example, if it is *your* job to call customers or prospects and schedule appointments for sharing the product(s), service(s), or opportunity you have to offer, and no one has been called, you know *who* is responsible! It's not for the sake of being punitive, but rather to be sure you are both doing whatever it takes to make your enterprise successful.

Second, it gives each spouse a sense of ownership in the business. It's fine to be able to say *we run our own business*. But unless each of you has real, operational responsibilities, saying *we run our own business* can become rather hollow. And this will reflect itself in the income, or lack of it, you generate from your business.

Finally, it's a matter of recognizing, acknowledging, and congratulating each other on the things one could and does accomplish better than the other. It helps you appreciate the contributions you each make. It isn't a contest, or even necessarily an even-handed task assignment.

It's important to realize early on that you each need well-defined responsibilities that allow each of you to have key roles in starting, building, and maintaining the business. Some roles may even be suitable for including your children's help in the business, based, of course, on their interests and abilities as well. You'll find certain divisions will be obvious, some will evolve, and some will ultimately become a co-arrangement.

Take us for example....

Aprill

The first major, ongoing responsibility I took on was the bookkeeping. I fought this idea, and was quite adamant in explaining why I wasn't the right person for the job. I was the girl who told everyone I majored in English so I wouldn't have to take any more math. I could not do it, did not want to do it, and thought I shouldn't *have* to do it.

But Chuck saw in me what most people, including myself, had never seen—a businesswoman. Because he knew me so well, he knew that no matter what adversity I met with, I

would guard *our* business and *our* family coffers like a ti-
gress guarding her cubs. And I couldn't contradict him on
that point. It was a strength only a spouse would be likely to
see. And it was the first of many times that we would be able
to show and allow the other to use talents, strengths, and
skills hitherto unknown to the *outside* world.

Some characteristics are so obvious that responsibility division is a no-brainer. For example, since Chuck had the
contacts, the expertise, and great sales savvy—business development fell to him. That did not mean I was to ignore any
opportunities I had to help us gain a client. It did not mean I
didn't have to go on any sales calls, or that I would never
take a phone call from a potential client. It just meant that
business development was one of *his* specialties. We decided
I could assist our business best in that area by following his
lead and giving him the moral, managerial, and clerical support he might need to be successful.

I decided to take on our business's financial management and administrative duties. And even though I'm
responsible for the day-to-day operations, I still ask Chuck
his opinion on insurance, investments and cash flow issues.
For example, I do comparative shopping on our health insurance every couple of years. After that, I ask Chuck what
he likes about our current plan, and share with him the
highlights of another plan I'm considering. He then gives
me his feedback, which I take into consideration. I then
make the final decision because doing such analyses is one
of the areas where I shine and can contribute something of
value to our business.

Because I'm a *detail-oriented* person, I don't mind paperwork, administrative forms, and general business management.
I am the best of the two of us for the job. It's not that Chuck
couldn't do it. He did it for two years before I joined him. But
now, I can do it and, as a result, he is free to use *his* real
strengths for the business.

Chuck

One of my greatest faults was that I believed nothing could be done as well as I could do it. *Nothing.* For example, I'm not a carpenter. I know nothing about carpentry, and have a hard time driving a nail, setting a screw or sanding a surface. Even so, I still believed that if I set my mind to building a four-poster bed that it would be the finest, most beautiful bed ever constructed!

So, you can probably imagine my initial thoughts on sharing responsibilities. They went something like this: "I'll be the president, CEO, CFO, creative director, sales manager, director of purchasing, production supervisor and quality control manager, and you do whatever is left!"

Plus, recognize that the person with whom I would share the responsibilities was the person I love and trust most in this world—Aprill. She had never given me any reason whatsoever to believe her judgment and decision-making abilities were anything short of stellar.

It was just, well, that I had trouble letting go of *control.* One of the reasons I started my (notice I said *my!*) own business was so *I* would be in charge—in control. And that meant *full* control. It honestly hadn't crossed my mind that Aprill, too, might want some control.

After all, I had been doing this for two years on my own. Sure, Aprill was a "principal investor," but I was running the company. Now, however, it had grown large enough and busy enough that Aprill could leave her job and we could work *together.* It was a great change and the accomplishment of one of our goals. Nevertheless, I needed to face letting go of some of that control or, I'd have too much to do and she wouldn't have anything to do! So, some of all the things I had been doing— selling the projects, creating the materials, managing the production, invoicing, collecting, balancing the books, purchasing the equipment, paying the vendors and the taxes, emptying the trash, and vacuuming the floor—needed to be done by Aprill.

You notice I said earlier that one of my greatest faults was that I believed nothing could be done as well as I could do it myself. What a burden that was!

Admittedly, there is still part of me that believes "if you want something done right you have to do it yourself." But I also now believe that if I want something done right I can ask Aprill to do it or help me with it. What a relief!

It's important to share responsibilities for another reason besides the fact that, when done effectively, each of you can use your strengths to their highest potential. It also (remember one of the naysayers?) keeps you from "killing each other!"

Aprill

What if Chuck and I had both shopped for a different long-distance carrier, and each of us had signed up with a different company—*without* telling the other? One of us would have to straighten the mess out, tell the carrier *they* picked "never mind," and realistically, may have even gotten upset with the other person.

Even though we rarely argue, we might have about that! But since I am the business manager, that kind of decision comes under my "umbrella." That doesn't mean Chuck doesn't express his opinion. But he trusts me (There's that operative word again!) to make the best final decision for our company and family.

Another reason to have designated roles is that it keeps your clients, or whomever you're communicating with, within or outside the structure of your business, from being confused. For example, when our clients have a project to discuss, they know to talk to Chuck. If they have an invoice to discuss, they talk to me. They figure this out very quickly by the way we work with them.

Clearly defined roles convey a sense of clarity, professionalism and service-orientation. And even if I have assisted in the writing of a package, or Chuck knows an invoice has been lost, we still direct the client to our project manager (Chuck) or our business manager (Aprill).

As with Most Things in Life, Few Things Are "Cast in Stone"

Responsibilities can change or evolve. In any business, especially a small one, flexibility is also important. The key is to be generally consistent and, if you aren't, to communicate clearly to all the people involved.

Although Chuck usually handles project production management, there may be ongoing projects that require blocks of time every day or every week for maintenance purposes. Chuck doesn't like maintenance and Aprill doesn't mind it. So, in such instances, she would be the one to handle the production management. If we're making such role adjustments, we'll quickly let the vendors and clients know in order to avoid confusion.

There are inevitably some responsibilities no on wants to take on totally. For example, neither one of us wants the entire responsibility of keeping our office cleaned, running all the errands, or filing. So we both pitch in. Some days even emptying the trash cans is a good reason for one of us to get away from the desk for a while. So that person does it. Besides which, nothing is beneath either of us!

Although Aprill handles most of the mail, sometimes running to the post office gives Chuck the chance to get out of the office for a much-needed fifteen-minute break. Similarly, Chuck usually takes proofs to and from our client and vendor offices. But, if he has other priorities with what he needs to do, Aprill does such deliveries and pickups. We simply do whatever it takes to make the business a success.

Chuck

One little thing we've done to make working together even more fun is to give ourselves titles. I am President,

Sales Manager, and Courier. Aprill is Executive Vice President, CFO, and Receptionist. Neither one of us has been brave enough to *give* or to *take* the title of Janitor! It's not that we don't recognize that as a valuable role—it's just that neither one of us particularly likes that job!

The point is, *focus on the positive rather than make a big deal over little things.* Suffice it to say that you'll work these things out as you go along. You care too much about your spouse, as well as your business, to let them get in the way of your happiness and success. If you temporarily slip into a negative attitude, have faith things will work out and move on from it. It's not worth stressing yourself out—it only makes you miserable.)

Division of responsibilities is essential. It shows you trust each other and builds on that trust. It helps you keep things running smoothly and frequently prevents tempers from flaring. You might even need to write out how you will divide your duties. We never did that, mainly because we need to remain somewhat flexible in the way we are set up. But think about what works best for you, then do it, however you may decide to go about it. Each couple's business and relationship is somewhat unique.

Questions to Ask Yourself...

There are many books written about finding your strengths, discovering your gifts, and doing what you love to do. And some are very good. They can help you reevaluate your life so you can identify your dream and go for it. People today are searching, more than ever, in an effort to move on and make their lives better.

Here are eight simple questions for you and your spouse to ask yourselves before you decide who does what in your business. They are general enough to apply to almost any industry. And again, the suggested questions are simply guidelines. You may need to adjust around them some, depending on the nature of what you're doing. For example, if you're in direct sales or associated with a network of others, a lot of these things may be set up for you, according to what has worked for others over the years. And due to the common elements in many businesses, they'll hold true in most cases.

You may not need reminding, but here it is anyway: Answer honestly! This is *your* life, *your* marriage and *your* business we're talking about. Let down your guard, dowse your ego, be real, swallow your pride and answer candidly. It's worth it, really! Then compare your answers with your spouse's, discuss the best way to go, and assign responsibilities. And remember, especially in the beginning, and also as you grow together, that you may want or need to change some of your original agreements. After all, it's *your* business!

Between you and your spouse...

1) Q. Who is the best money manager?

A. This spouse is probably the best person to handle the money in your business. He or she would be the one to select your method of keeping records and choose your bank and the services you need. Ideally, they would also handle your household finances.

2) Q. Who is most at ease, face-to-face, especially with new people?

A. This spouse is probably the best person to handle outside sales. He or she would need some training in sales if they aren't already savvy in this area.

3) Q. Who is the best under pressure?

A. This spouse is probably the person best suited to handle any scheduling or trafficking responsibilities your business may require.

4) Q. Who is the best negotiator?

A.This spouse would probably have the responsibility for purchasing, and could most efficiently head up any long- or short-term contract negotiations you may have.

5) Q. Who is most public relations oriented?

A. This spouse could probably best accept the role of president (or chief executive officer), at least from a public perspective.

6) Q. Who enjoys working on the phone the most?

A. This is a good indicator of who would be best to answer the phone, and be involved in introductory sales contacts. (It is recommended that the CEO and the person who answers the phone *not* be the same person, if possible.)

7) Q. Who is the best strategist or planner?

A. This spouse would be the best to take the lead in determining the long-term focus of your company. He or she would obviously solicit and accept input from the other spouse, but should accept both responsibility and accountability for the direction the company needs to head. This would be the spouse who assumes the strongest leadership role in your business.

8) Q. Who has the best sense of people's character, intentions, and how to deal with them?

A. This spouse would make all final hiring decisions, and would be involved in evaluating clients before entering into long-term contractual arrangements. In most cases, this will not be the best person to be in charge of sales.   (Salespeople, in general, are notorious for being enthusiastic beyond the point of distraction when it comes to the *goodness* of people to whom they are endeavoring to sell!)

Chapter 5

———— ❧ ————

Money Matters

How to Handle Finances Without Going Emotionally Broke

Moving Out of the Financial "Box"

Statistics show that more marital misunderstandings, disagreements and conflicts occur over money than anything else. This includes how to raise children, where to live, and even sex!

Money—and the things it will buy—has become the scorecard by which most people judge who wins and who loses. How much does he make compared to me? What kind of car does she drive compared to mine? How large is their home compared to ours?

However, it wasn't always this way. Before the industrial revolution, most people didn't think much about success. Their focus was on *survival*—having a place to live, food to eat and clothes to wear. How come that was so? The reasons are twofold:

First, the world was just not very mobile back then. It wasn't uncommon to be born, live your entire life and die without ever venturing more than 50 miles from home. Many times, families lived in the same houses which were passed down through the years from parents and grandparents before.

Second, the world offered very little communication. Newspapers were periodical (instead of daily), and they covered mostly *news*. There were few features or lifestyle stories and no stock market reports. Most people did not know how other people lived or how much money they earned. By and large, you weren't measured by your income at all. It was just considered a fact of life and you simply learned to live within those bounds, i.e., within your means.

As the twentieth century charged into full swing, the industrial revolution changed everything. People left childhood homes and areas where generations of the same family had lived—and moved to larger cities for employment. The promises of higher-paying jobs and better lifestyles were the lures.

As the century progressed, communications became more advanced. Radio, then television, cable television and finally the Internet made sending and receiving information something that could be done at anytime, from anywhere, by anyone. You can be traveling in Australia or somewhere else and, as long as you can access the Internet, you can monitor weather anywhere else in the world!

What does all that have to do with your business's finances? Everything! Why are you in or thinking about going into business in the first place? Your answer may go something like this—*"To gain more control over my life, to spend more time with my spouse and family, to do the things I really want to do, to earn a better living and, hopefully, earn a lot of money!"*

Most money conflicts did not occur in marriages until couples saw, heard, and understood the power, comfort and satisfaction that can come with having lots of it. Once people became better traveled and more informed, the *haves* and the *have-nots* seemed to move further and further apart.

And the challenges of striving to go from one group to the other (or simply to maintain your position in the group you are already in) have grown as well—on the competitive and sometimes cutthroat job scene. This is especially true for those who have discovered that job security and loyalty toward employees is virtually nonexistent, as compared to historically, when it was the norm to be a "lifer" with the same company.

If you are not careful, you can fall into a very common trap: *how much money you make, and how much money you have—compared to when you worked for someone else—will become your gauge for how successful your business is.* Know that this is simply not a reliable barometer. If you focus on this false indicator, any challenges your marriage has suffered over money *before* you worked together could pale in comparison to those you could suffer *when* you work together. "Keeping your day job," as you build your business, can help you get over this hurdle and certainly avoid a lot of financial stress.

Keeping Finances in Their Proper Place
Here is a hidden truth that is applicable whether you are in or starting a business with your spouse, or simply endeavoring to live happily ever after as a married couple: *Money is nothing more than the tool you use to finance your lifestyle and fund your dreams.*

Sounds simple, doesn't it? Well, it *is* simple, regardless of how some people may seem to complicate it. Remember, money is *not* the goal. And it is not smart to elevate it to such a level of importance that you place it before your personal satisfaction, your family obligations or your marital responsibilities. Money is purely a *tool*. You use it. It is the fuel for your *lifestyle*. It is not meant to be the fuel for your *life!*

Keeping money in the proper perspective and managing it in a professional manner can be a contributing factor to your success. Although that, alone, will not ensure your success. However, not having the perspective that money is just a tool, and mismanaging it, will almost certainly result in failure.

With that in mind, here are some key points that have helped us be successful in managing our finances. And they can work for you too.

Make Someone Responsible

For the first nine years of our marriage, before starting our business, Chuck managed the household money. He paid the bills and mortgage, balanced the checkbook, invested what was possible, saved for vacations, and everything else. When he started the business, I still had my job and my salary paid all the bills. So, at that point, it made sense for me to take over handling the household finances. I began paying the bills and mortgage, balancing the checkbook, and managing any extra spending money. Chuck continued to handle investments (retirement savings) and the business financial transactions. He enjoyed it and had a special knack for it.

This was a good formula for us. Chuck was operating the new business and he had the best perspective on how he wanted to make our money work for the business. So he managed that aspect of our finances. He kept me informed, and came to me for financial assistance when major purchases needed to be made, or when we needed to infuse operating capital into our new business.

I was now running the monetary aspect of the household. I told Chuck how much money was coming in, how much was in the bank, and what was available for investment in the new company.

Someone was responsible for certain things. And that leads to something else—accountability.

Make Both of You Accountable

It's not enough to just be responsible. Responsibility must be linked with accountability.

We're not talking about employing strong-arm tactics of investigation and punishment. We're only suggesting that when you give each other the responsibility for managing certain aspects of your finances, part of this responsibility is agreeing to have accountability.

The easiest—and most painless—form of accountability is pure, simple communication! Letting each other know what is happening qualifies as accountability. If you manage the home finances and know that an annual insurance payment is coming due, depending on the amount of the bill and your monetary situation, you may need to talk about it and plan for how you are going to pay it.

If your spouse manages your investments and knows the date your pension-related deposits have to be made, you may need to talk about it and plan for it. Or, when you have a seminar or convention you need to attend, for which tickets need to be purchased, you may need to discuss what it will take to accomplish that.

An important recommendation: Make the following pledge to each other in the beginning, and it will help you head off financial problems "at the pass" if they occur. Now face each other, raise your right hands and repeat:

"I promise to keep you informed regarding the areas of our finances for which I am responsible, I will trust you to make good decisions in the areas for which you are responsible, and I will not become offended, defensive, or angry when you approach me with questions regarding decisions I have made or are about to make regarding finances. If I do so, I give you permission to bring it to my attention, and I will learn from my inappropriate response, let it go, and move on with a positive attitude. So help me!"

Believe us. This pledge (or one like it) can save you a lot of grief if money-related issues arise. And, unless you've already got total financial freedom, i.e., have all the money you need and want, you're likely to have some discussions about your finances!

You May Want to Automate
When he set up the business system, Chuck chose an automated, computer bookkeeping program. It continues to prove to be one of his best business decisions.

Computer accounting programs offer simple, easy-to-use debit/credit systems that are similar in content and operation to those used by every Fortune 500 company. Since our business is simple, our accounting system has a lot of features we still don't use. More traditional businesses, however, could benefit from things like inventory reports, orders, invoicing, and payroll.

Your business may or may not need an accounting program. For example, in the direct selling industry, the corporate suppliers often take orders directly from the distributors (usually independent businessowners) and customers/clients via catalog, toll-free telephone number, or e-commerce. So many of these responsibilities, i.e., inventory, invoicing, and distributor compensation, are handled by the suppliers.

For those of you who could use even the simplest checking account system, there are any number of good programs available. The bestselling one is probably the Quicken group of products. The most important message is this: almost every business can operate more smoothly and profitably with a computer driven bookkeeping and accounting system. It makes keeping track of finances practically foolproof—so much so that even an English major can do it!

With the computer, day-to-day accounting is simpler. Plus, it makes tax time a virtual breeze. Setting your business up on the computer will pay for itself many times over in terms of the amount of headaches and time you can save.

Consolidate as Much as Possible

Once I joined the business full-time, I took over both the home and business finances. Again, it just made sense. My taking on the additional financial responsibilities with the business allowed Chuck to concentrate on selling and producing our product.

This required some major adjustments on both our parts. As you continue in your business, you'll learn more and more that flexibility is essential!

Chuck

The most challenging thing I needed to do was to turn over the financial management of our business to Aprill. Prior to that, I had always managed our money. I made all of the decisions. We had always discussed money and I had always kept her informed about how well (or poorly) we were doing financially. As she mentioned, I had already turned over the home finances to her a couple of years before. Even though I hated paying bills and balancing the checkbook, I still felt uneasy about not having the *control*.

Would she be able to do it? *I was sure she could do it.* Would she be able to do it right? *Well, what do you consider right?* Would she continue to do it just like I did it? *Probably not.*

Then one day, like a bolt out of the blue, it hit me. I trusted Aprill to take care of our best interests. Why would she do anything to hurt us? Even though control sounded like a good thing, to tell you the truth, it was really a heavy burden. Trust is *much* better than control. It allows us to share the handling of our challenging tasks.

Since that day, I've never questioned how Aprill manages our finances. And for me to say that is a monumental step compared to where I was in the past.

Aprill

As I said earlier, I did not want to take over the business finances. I didn't trust myself to do it, and certainly didn't know why Chuck would want me to do it. But, because Chuck is sometimes also known as the Great Persuader, he showed me how it was the most rational arrangement for us. He really knows my buttons.

My distaste and reluctance for this responsibility (and accountability!) far exceeded three months. It may have gone on for more like three years. He had done a great job with our finances, and I knew I could not do as good a job or do it like he did. Why? Because we have different styles.

But I did do it. And even though I didn't handle it just like Chuck would have, we still survived. In fact, during some periods, we even thrived. We've managed to make every tax payment and Keogh (pension) contribution, and we've never missed paying a bill. We've even been able to have a little fun and a few vacations. I've also had periods when I wanted to cry my eyes out because I couldn't somehow turn $1,000 into $10,000 (and I would think it must be all my fault!). But through Chuck's encouragement and my self-induced pep talks and tongue lashings, I've sloshed through the muck and mire and turned it into a responsibility I at least don't dread.

Although keeping the company books sometimes tests my character and faith, I've startled myself into believing I can do it. And better yet, my husband, business partner, and head cheerleader *trusts* me to do it.

Now I handle all receipts and disbursements for both our business and home. Chuck lets me know if there is a big business purchase that needs to be made and how soon we need to make it. At that point, he is depending on me to prepare us financially for that transaction. I remind him if we need to invoice a client as soon as possible to improve cash flow. If there are no invoices to send, it is up to me to arrange the month's expenses around the current cash flow.

Sometimes it's really challenging. There are times when I feel the need to remind Chuck that a weekend getaway may not be financially feasible, and there are times he needs to remind me of all the projects that will be ready to invoice next month. So, somehow it all works out!

Chuck Continued—*If It Ain't Broke...*

Aprill is a better money manager than I am. Soon after consolidating the home and business finances, she fashioned a budget (something we'd never done before) and a simple system to keep track of our spending. This was so that neither of us could ask incredulously, *"Where did all our money go?"* (as many couples do, whether they are in business together, or not).

We developed a personal expense sheet as well as one for monthly household expenses. And while we're still not strict budget keepers, we are each responsible enough to keep track of things on our own. But some people, as they may each juggle a job while building a business with their spouse, will need to make a special effort to keep accurate records.

As she shared, I am a better investor than Aprill. Fruitful investing requires research, tracking, and a certain intuition. I enjoy it, and have had a fair amount of success at it. Therefore, it made sense for me to continue managing our investments, as well as our pension plans and other retirement vehicles.

I check with Aprill to see how much money is available for investing and when, and then I make the appropriate decisions. Aprill reviews all the transactions, and keeps the records so she can stay informed on the progress and status of all our investments (consistent with her role as primary manager of all finances).

Aprill

Even though Chuck continues to be in charge of the investment decisions, it is still up to me to judge when and what amount will be contributed to the nonretirement investments. (Chuck reminds me that it is my nature to keep the money where I can *see* it!)

When the money comes out of the ordinary household expense, such as a special contribution at church, I review the figures with him to make sure we are in agreement as a couple. We don't argue over money. We never did, even before we started our business. I think when it comes to finances, the key is to trust, respect, and honor each other in the process. Sound familiar?

The point is, even though it is good to consolidate as much of the financial responsibilities with one person as possible, only do it if it'll contribute to your greater success. If one of you is particularly adept at one aspect of financial management, and enjoys doing it, keep at it. Remember, one of the reasons you're starting or operating your own business is to have more control over your life. And part of control means doing what you each want to do as much as possible.

Home Expenses Are Not Office Expenses and Office Expenses Are Not Home Expenses

Make the line between business expenses and personal finances very distinct. For example, our personal savings account is used for personal *extras* (just like yours probably is). And we do not use business savings for vacation money.

If you are a sole proprietorship, the business is listed under either one of your names and you can take owner draws (paychecks) from the business as you need them, depending on the profitability of the business. And if you go on to incorporate, each of you can draw a salary and take bonuses from the business, once you are profitable enough to do so, of course!

There are advantages and disadvantages to operating as a sole proprietorship and each of the various forms of corporations. You could also choose to be a partnership—which has its own pros and cons. Many, especially initially, prefer the simplicity of a sole proprietorship. However, there are many books already written on the topic, so we won't go into that here. If you have general questions, your mentor or leader may be able to help you. For answers to more specific questions, ask your accountant. You don't have one? Well...

You May Need to Hire an Accountant

In some cases, especially when you are in a business like franchising or direct sales, you probably already have in place a well-thought-out system of success to follow. So, in the beginning, unless you're numbers oriented and in tune with the tax laws because of the work you do, all you may need is a good end-of-the-year tax service. You're also likely to have leaders and mentors to guide you as you go along—consider their recommendations seriously.

If you don't already have an accountant, you may want to hire one as your business grows. An accountant is one of the three key financial relationships many businesspeople find they need to make operating their business a simpler, more enjoyable endeavor. They can help you save a lot of money.

An accountant would be able to help you set up and understand your bookkeeping system, help you through tax times paperwork, and alert you to new rules and regulations. They could also suggest retirement savings vehicles for your particular situation, handle tax questions, and countless other concerns that are likely to come up as your business grows and becomes more profitable.

Finding an excellent accountant can be easy. Ask your friends, your mentor or leader, or other business associates the name of their accountant, and what they like about him or her. Then talk to a few accountants. Decide which one you think will work best with you and go with that person. You can always change later if it doesn't work out.

Most people who have never worked with an accountant see accounting as black and white. Actually, the practice of accounting is very gray. So it is especially important to find an accountant who understands and honors your personal ethics.

When we hired our accountant, we told all candidates that our accounting requirements were simple. We wanted every tax advantage we were due, but nothing that could be questioned. In short, if it was spelled out in black and white, we'd take it. If it was gray, we'd prefer to stay away from it.

It was important to us that, if we were ever audited, we would not lose even one minute of sleep wondering if the tax people would find *this* or notice *that*. We wanted to operate to the letter of the law. And especially when the letter was in our favor, we definitely wanted to take full advantage of it. Bring on those deductions!

Also, note that finding a great accountant and sticking with them for a long time can reduce your work load even further. As your accountant becomes familiar with your business, your bookkeeping practices, your software, and your basic financial situation, each year becomes easier and easier. We have had the same accountant for several years. We're happy with his service and his pricing.

That leads us to another important aspect—negotiate fees with your accountant based on how *you* want to work with him or her. When you start your business, it will probably seem like you'll need to talk with your accountant every day for the rest of your life. You won't. Unless your business grows at an astronomical rate (and it could!), you'll soon be able to answer most of your own questions. It's best to find an accountant who will work with you on an hourly basis (as opposed to a retainer). Our accountant actually bills us one time each year after tax season. He keeps track of how often we talk with him throughout the year, and gives us one bill. That in itself makes his and our bookkeeping easier!

An excellent accountant is as valuable as an excellent banker...

Find an Excellent Banker
Chuck

My father was self-employed almost his entire working life, doing business with the same bank. In fact, he still banks there in his retirement.

I remember him telling me about Luther, the bank president. Occasionally, Luther would call him and say "Do you need anything? Need to borrow some money?" Or, if my father needed to make any type of transaction at all, he'd call Luther, and Luther would take care of it.

By the time we opened our business, we were fully into the age of ATMs (automatic teller machines), and telephone and Internet banking. I didn't even know the name of the manager of the mega-bank branch at which we did business. Still, we knew that if we were to be successful in the business we chose, we needed to have a banker...like Luther.

Again, this will vary depending on the business you are building. Some people find that they can support their business with their employment income—at least until they can transition to working fulltime in their business—without jeopardizing their finances.

Aprill

Chuck opened our first business banking accounts and did his best to establish a relationship with the branch manager. We knew that, as business owners in our industry, this was an important step for us to make to prepare for the potential future financial needs that could arise. This particular manager was nice enough, but that was about all. There was no proactivity on his part to serve us, other than in an unimaginative rudimentary way. He showed no willingness or desire to learn our business or our potential financial needs.

So, when I joined the company, we changed branches. We called the manager at the new branch, and that same afternoon he came to our office, found out all our needs (present and projected), brought back all of the necessary paperwork and began establishing our fine relationship with his branch. In short, he gave us the personal customer service we wanted and needed, but had no idea still existed.

Not Mr. Drysdale

Most of us have lost the concept of *the banker*. Our mental image of a banker may be Mr. Drysdale from *The Beverly Hillbillies* or Mr. Potter from *It's a Wonderful Life*. Sure, most of us meet with bank employees now and then to apply for a mortgage, get new car financing, or obtain a safe deposit box. But, for the most part, we bank with a logo, not a person. And we have little loyalty to the logo—stopping at virtually any ATM across the country to get cash when and where we need it.

Fine, customer-oriented bankers *do* still exist, even in this high-tech age. Find yourself one. You may need to change banks if you are unhappy with the service you are currently receiving. Or, you may be able to go to another branch, explain to the manager your dissatisfaction with your old branch, and discover what he or she can offer instead.

A banker can help you set up the accounts you need, and get rid of those you don't. He or she can assist you in reducing your fees by grouping accounts into special packages. Your banker can help you obtain financing for your major purchases, or secure loans for operating capital.

We make it a point to meet with our banker each year. Even though we are in a business with unpredictable annual revenues, we have been able to obtain a line of credit, and increase the limit on the line every year. We have only the accounts we need, and we pay very few fees. On the rare occasions when we've had account service challenges, we have had someone to call and take care of the situation.

Having a dependable banker has significantly decreased our money worries and concerns. And when that's the case, your partnership as business owners—and husband and wife—is less stressed and much happier.

There is one other relationship that can prove invaluable...

Find a Reputable Insurance Agent

How much you make, how much you spend or invest, and how much you have left over are only part of excellent financial management. As business owners and, more importantly, as co-owners of the family business that may be solely responsible for the financial well-being of you and your family, being properly insured is crucial.

Aprill

Since I was an insurance agent when Chuck first started the business, I wrote the business owners insurance, and got our health and disability insurance in order. If you don't already have disability insurance, be a considerate spouse and get some! When you are a business owner, this coverage becomes more important than ever, because it's likely your family depends on your health, or compensation for lack of it, more than ever. Actually, it's best to have all your personal insurance in order *before* you even begin working with your spouse.

I know a couple who each assumed the other had taken care of the health insurance. As it turned out, the wife had actually not been covered for six months because of this lack of communication.

It is important for one of you to take the responsibility for making sure all your insurance bases are covered. Can you imagine the heartache, guilt and pain if a calamity struck and you weren't covered by insurance when you easily could have been? Love, respect, and honor each other enough to get this job done.

Insurance Can Be Complicated

A reputable insurance agent can help you. You may even have insurance available through your corporate supplier(s). We actually work with three different agents. Insurance is a very specialized field, and not every agent will be capable of giving you both service and selection.

Some of the policies you may want to consider are:

♥ Major Medical Health Insurance. At the bare minimum, purchase catastrophic health insurance to ensure your family against a long-term, financially debilitating illness of one of your family members.

♥ Urgent Care Insurance. If you can afford it, urgent care insurance can take care of all of your health needs. Regular check-ups, pre- and post-natal care, and emergency care are all included. HMOs (Health Maintenance Organizations), PPOs (Preferred Provider Organizations), and other forms of urgent care insurance are available with varying deductibles, levels of coverage, limits, and costs.

♥ Life Insurance. You and your spouse need to have adequate life insurance. This is especially important if you have children. The loss of one spouse has obvious emotional impact on the family. But the loss of one member of your new (or not so new) entrepreneurial team could greatly impact the future financial well-being of your business, and your family. (This largely depends on how your business is set up and whether your income from it continues without both of you being present.) Life insurance can offer you peace of mind and is available in a variety of amounts. And depending on the type of policy you choose, it can be remarkably affordable.

♥ Disability Insurance. Although the death of a spouse might be considered more traumatic, there is also the possibility that one spouse might become disabled. You and your spouse will want to be covered for both short- and long-term disability. (For those of you who have disability coverage on your job, remember: it won't cover you while you're at your family business location or elsewhere as you're doing activities associated with your business.)

Putting It All Together

You need to consider very carefully how to properly manage your finances. Sometimes that means respecting the other's financial point of view, even when it is very different from your own!

Aprill

I see our finances day to day, week to week, month to month. I know when our accounts are low and just how low they are. I also know what bills are due, when they're due and how much we owe. I know our receivables picture to the penny and day, and what it means to the current expenses picture.

Chuck is more of the big picture man. He knows when our profits are better than the last year's, what billables are in progress, and his sales projections. I'm into the details of how much do we have today, and he is more interested in how much we will have tomorrow.

It took some adjustments on both our parts, but we've discovered that both points of view are equally important to the financial health of our business. I've learned not to panic immediately when the cash flow is low. And, as a result, Chuck understands me when I get serious and give him spending warnings for a certain period of time!

On the other hand, when I worry about quarterly tax payments or pension contributions based on current numbers, Chuck is quick to show me the year-to-date numbers and convince me what can and will be done. As a result, we have come to depend on each other's instincts and savvy. We *trust and support* each other.

Chapter 6

———— ❤ ————

It's 7 a.m. Already—
Why Aren't You Up?

How to Handle Differences in Work Styles

What Would Your Ideal Schedule Look Like?

Say you could set your alarm clock, the clock where you work, and the clock in your car, to your biological clock. Then also imagine you could then function just the way you want to on your own schedule—without worrying about how the rest of the world would react. What would your schedule be?

Would you go to sleep around midnight or 1 a.m. and get up between 8 a.m. and 9 a.m.? Would you start work at 10 p.m. (like a graphic designer we know), work until 7 a.m., see the children off to school, sleep eight hours, then greet your children when they get off the school bus?

Maybe you would run your life like a computer programmer we once knew. He was single, and worked three 12-hour shifts a week on three consecutive days. The other 12 hours of those days he ate and slept. Then, he had a four-day weekend every week. Or would you be like the printer who arranged with his employer to work seven days for 14 hours a day, then take seven days off? How about the schedule of the couple in direct sales who play with their children during the day and share their opportunity, products, and services in the evenings?

One of the benefits of self-employment is having some flexibility in choosing when you work. Once you start your business (if you haven't already done so), you may be able to get closer to working when your biological clock tells you you're most productive. This could set a better tone for your whole day. And, when you bring your spouse into the picture, it could prove even more interesting.

Your spouse—who may already be your new business partner—could have a biological clock that isn't set the same as yours. Or your spouse may have a biological clock that is set *exactly the same* as yours. So what could such scenarios mean? After all, now there isn't just a family to maintain, there is also a business to build and run. Let's take a look at Stan and Sheila...

Stan and Sheila

Sheila is someone who functions best in the morning. Under deadline pressure, she can go into the office at 6 a.m. and, many times, get the job done by the time Stan arrives between 9:30 and 10 a.m. Sometimes she resents this.

On the other hand, Stan is not particularly thrilled when Sheila is ready to call it a day by 4 p.m. "Besides," Stan thinks to himself, "Sheila should know by now that even if I came in at 6 a.m., it would do no one any good." At 2 p.m. he often looks up to find Sheila fighting a losing battle with the *after-lunch sleepies*. He shakes his head in disbelief, in high gear himself, and carries on with the business at hand.

Deciding that letting such resentments build was not good for their business or personal relationship, so they decided to talk about it over lunch one day. Simply acknowledging to each other that their productivity times seemed out of sync took away a lot of the pressure and gave them an opportunity to work through the challenges this presented. They wrote out what time of day they felt most focused on the business, the times of day the family required their focus, and the times of day when focus just wasn't going to happen.

Now, when there is business she needs to take care of right away, Sheila gets an early start, while Stan gets the children off to school. He also unloads the dishwasher, starts the laundry, and does some of the other light housekeeping as necessary. Then, when Stan is still working away at 6 p.m., Sheila runs to the grocery, gets dinner for the family, and checks homework. They both take care of baths and bedtimes for the children, then enjoy some quiet time the rest of the evening.

When Sheila and Stan both need to work early and late, and deal with household chores and family obligations, they need to sacrifice relaxation time in the evening. But knowing what to expect from each other has taken a lot of stress out of their lives, and has helped make both their marriage and business more successful.

You Say *Tomato*; I Say *Tomahto*

When a husband and wife work together, there are going to be some differences in opinion. One of you may want classic, traditional oak office furniture while the other might want contemporary glass and stainless steel. You may prefer darker offices with accent lighting while your spouse may like bright, fluorescent light. Your spouse may like felt-tip pens while you may prefer to use nothing but pencils.

Fortunately, most of these differences are related to style and not substance. (We'll address style differences in depth in Chapter 8.) This isn't the case with productivity timetables, however.

Manage your respective times of highest productivity, and focus your energy during those times on your business activities. Understand and accept that there's bound to be some differences between you in this area. This is crucial to the ultimate success of your business.

Our experience is similar to Stan's and Sheila's.

We aren't on the same biological clock. For example, one of us works better in the morning, and the other in the afternoon. Does this bother us now? Hardly ever. We do our best to use our differences to our advantage.

Whether you are building and running a business from your home or an outside location, full-time or part-time, your maximum productivity times do not have to be the same for your business to be successful. And besides which, as you both grow and develop new practices, your maximum productivity times may change. Just be flexible and do whatever it takes to make both your marriage and business successful and happy.

Let's say you've started building your new business and are working it part-time while you both continue full-time at your current jobs. And, for the sake of this illustration, let's say one of you is a morning person. It probably would be pretty easy for that person to get started one, maybe even two hours earlier than normal and devote those hours to your new business. The other spouse, at the same time, can follow his or her regular routine, which may include getting the children ready for school, packing lunches, and so forth. If you have small children, that may be the quietest time of day in your home. And if you have teenage children, you may not be able to get into any of the bathrooms anyway, so why not work?

Or, let's suppose early evenings are more productive for one of you. Let that person focus on the business, perhaps make some calls to prospective clients or associates, while the other one gets dinner and takes care of homework and bath time for the children.

Both of you need to be observant of the times of the day where you are more easily productive in your business than at other times. This will be true regardless of whether you are a full- or part-time business owner. But there is not much time for either of you to be inactive, especially in the first couple of years, as you build your business. So self-discipline is definitely a must as you do your business activities, even during those times when your energy level may not be at its peak.

What you may be doing at 8:30 a.m. (emptying the dishwasher, walking the dogs, getting the children off to school), may not be directly productive for your business, but may be essential to your household and your family. Maintenance jobs like opening the mail, calling or running for office supplies, or going to the bank may not feel as vital as making sales calls, but these are all tasks that need to be done. An excellent balance between maintenance chores and business building activities is essential as you both strive to work along with your biological clocks as much as you can.

Don't Force It—With Your Own Business, You Won't Generally Have To!
Aprill

Work in tune with your biological clock as much as possible Be aware, though, in the beginning when one or both of you may have full-time jobs, and you're building your business on the side, you may need to be very creatively flexible. You may need to take short "power naps," a quick walk, or do something else to rev yourself up when you don't feel like doing whatever it takes to build and run your business. We'll talk more about this in a bit.

Here are some of our experiences:

When I was an insurance agent, I quickly learned that, due to my biological clock, I needed to schedule my sales calls, whenever possible, after lunch. That meant that sometimes I chose to stay at the office into the evening to make those calls. It was extremely difficult for me to get in the sales groove in the mornings.

Now when I start working around 10 a.m., Chuck is in the middle of his sales calls. Most of the time I wave to him, plug in my laptop, and stick my head into my accounting duties for an hour or so. I've learned I need something that can be done quietly and efficiently to get going. Chuck is going as soon as his feet hit the floor, but is winding down by 4 p.m., unless he has a heavy workload that day; then he keeps on going.

Chuck

I was never a child who had to be dragged out of bed. And, unlike most kids I knew, I never had a set bedtime. When I was in second or third grade, I got sleepy around 8:30 or 9 p.m., and I went to bed. I had to get up around 7 a.m. to make it to school and I did.

In college I took the earliest classes, without reservation. I loved to have all of my classes out of the way before lunch if possible. I worked in my dormitory's post office and I always wanted the earliest morning shift. I could get all of the mail sorted and put into the boxes, and have a little extra time to read the morning newspaper—all before my first class!

That early riser attribute has carried over into my professional life. In the two companies I worked for prior to starting our business, I was always the first person to arrive in the morning. I could accomplish more in the hour to hour and a half before everyone arrived than I could throughout the rest of the day. I never intended to be a morning person, but nonetheless I'm good at it!

The First Key

Realize everyone operates differently and capitalize on those differences.

There are times you may feel lazy, staying in bed an hour after your spouse hits the floor running. There may be other times when you feel like you are not pulling your weight because your productivity times aren't in sync. But while there are some advantages to having more or less the same high productivity times, there are distinct advantages with different times, too. Whatever your situation is, you can make it all work for you and what you're endeavoring to accomplish with your business.

The Second Key

Be willing to compromise and adapt your preferences to serve the needs of your particular business.

In many cases, at least in the U.S., it is still a 9 to 5 world. Depending on your business, this may not present a challenge. But if it does, work together to make the necessary compromises that will ensure you the best chance for success.

Build and manage your business in a way that works best for both your biological clocks, as much as possible. (This will also be true if and when you bring any employees on board.) After all, that's probably one of the reasons you started a business together—to be in control of your own schedule, instead of your schedule being in control of you, right?

Turning Disadvantage Into Advantage:

This is simple and can be a lot of fun.

Each of you keeps track of the highest productivity times you're experiencing in your business. Do this for a couple of weeks. Write down the things you did and when you did them. Then compare notes with your spouse.

Next, make a list of the advantages you have because of the timing of your biological clocks. You may be saying, "But they're different and this causes us more disadvantages than advantages." Okay, what now? Go ahead and list the disadvantages you perceive you have as a result of your different high-productivity periods.

Let's look at an example: Tom and Mary are building a home-based direct sales business, in addition to both of them working full-time at their jobs. They have two children. Besides sharing their products and services, they also share their opportunity with others who have a dream they'd like to make come true through generating additional income.

Mary functions best in the evening and early at night. Whereas, Tom is a morning person. Tom finds that he is easily able to get up a little earlier to have breakfast with a prospective client. Mary has a regular routine with the children before school, which she can handle alone before work, while Tom's out at breakfast on business.

So, that still leaves the evening and early night when Mary would be perky and Tom may be a bit less than his best. They decided that the children would quietly do homework before dinner, while Tom takes a 45-minute power nap to rejuvenate. Then, after dinner he could more effectively make some business telephone calls and, as needed, they could both get together with people to show their marketing and sales plan and share their products and services.

So, how can you and your spouse take a perceived disadvantage and turn it into an advantage? Take each disadvantage you listed and take a fresh approach. List the potential solutions and then take action. People who are successful, in any arena, go forward with whatever they've got to work with, and persist through any challenges they encounter—going straight for their goals. This principle of doing whatever it takes applies to all couples in their marriage-based businesses too!

Chances are excellent you can turn what you may have thought were *disadvantages* into what actually turns out to be *advantages* that benefit not just your business, but your entire life. Isn't that great?

Chapter 7

———❥———

Did You Turn the Copier Off?

Yes, You Can Still Take a Vacation and Even Have Some Fun!

It's Great to Know You Are Not Indispensable

It's human nature to think that the companies we work for revolve around our jobs. We may believe our part in the day-to-day operations is not only needed, but is also key to their success. Without the part we play, the entire mechanism of the company—the services we provide or the flow from raw materials to a delivered, finished product—would certainly grind to a halt, wouldn't they?

If we take even one day off, everyone will arrive, punch the clock, then look around and say, "Where is Joe? We cannot possibly produce our product (or render our services) without Joe." Management would call an emergency meeting, suspend operations for the day, and send everyone home without pay. Then, they would call your home and leave a message that, even though they hope your day off was pleasant, they must have you back the next day or the company will surely fold.

We don't think so!

Chuck

I used to believe I was indispensable to my last company, certain no one would know what to do if I wasn't there. The truth is, the company hardly noticed when I was gone! In fact, they hardly noticed when *anyone* was gone. Systems were in place and people knew their roles. And although we were always quite busy, everyone could step things up 10 or 20 percent in short bursts to cover for someone who was out for a day or even a week or two.

And not one time in 10 years did I return from vacation to find an "Out of Business" sign on the company's front door!

Taking a vacation when you work for a large company can be as easy as requesting the time, and taking it. You might have some extra work to do to get ready and some extra work to do when you return. But, in most cases, you can get up, turn the light off, close the door and go. And most importantly, when you return there will be a paycheck waiting for you—just like you'd been there all along.

But that's not how it is when you start your own business. You need to focus on your goals and delay gratification. You need to grow your business before you can reap its rewards.

Aprill

Since we have been in business together, we have enjoyed some of our best vacations—but not until after things were humming along. There is one picture of Chuck, taken during a Florida trip, that we often talk about. It's when we still worked for someone else in different companies. Sometimes he looks at it and says, "I can still remember exactly how I felt that day, and I know I will never feel that way again as long as we have our own business."

Actually, I think I know exactly what he means, because I have felt it too. When you work for someone else, you know that while you're away, people are piling papers on your desk, or someone is not handling your clients or work station as you would like. But the business still keeps going. However, if you have a business with no employees or associates to do things while you're gone, your business is basically closed.

Orders may be filled and delivered, invoices processed and paid by clients, direct mail pieces get printed and mailed. But this is probably all from arrangements you made *prior* to taking the time off. Clients can't reach you immediately if they feel the need, the phone can only record voice mail to be retrieved later and, possibly, opportunities could be lost.

But Is Paradise Really Lost?

So what do you do? Forget about a family vacation because "It's just impossible"? Spend vacation time from your full-time job working on your own business?

Are your children begging you to go to the beach? Is it bad for your marriage not having time away with your spouse?

There are examples through the ages of humans drawing away from their everyday lives for rest and relaxation. Even the American pioneers, who were a tremendous example of hard work and perseverance, would go on family camping trips to a special spot by a spring, or to visit family back east.

But how do you carve out a vacation when your business, and perhaps your job(s), require so much time?

Recreation Is Re-creation

Getting away is not just something many people *want* to do—it is something they feel they *need* to do. But it needs to be earned first, much like it does when you work for someone else. You don't start work one day and take a week's vacation the next, now do you?

It is always easy to rationalize a vacation:

- ♥ You and your family believe you deserve it.

- ♥ It's a family tradition to go to the beach in July, and you can't let business get in the way of that.

♥ If you don't get away, you believe you are in danger of exploding and everyone nearby will catch your wrath.

This is an easy game to play, as you can certainly create your own personal rationalizations. But once you've built your business to a reasonable level, you won't need to *rationalize* taking a vacation. You can then afford to take time away from your business to recharge your batteries and unwind—as a reward for accomplishing something.

When you start a new business you need to use your time as wisely as possible—to set yourself up for success. You need to take care of your business first, before it can take care of you! You need to start thinking like a businessperson.

Besides which, when you truly love what you do, it is fun for you and you probably won't crave vacations like you may do now. When you have more control over your life via your own business, you'll also have more options and feel less of a need to get away. And when you love what you do, you'll never have to work another day in your life again!

Start thinking like this regarding vacations:

♥ It's just not the right time. We'll go next year, after we accomplish...

♥ I'd love to, but this project needs to get done before we leave.

♥ If we spend that time working on the business, we'll be that much further along.

♥ We can't afford to take a week; let's do some afternoons.

♥ Let's look at ways we could blend business and pleasure.

The point is, when you start your own business with your spouse, you need to work now and play later.

Why? Taking a vacation requires time and money, which are particularly precious in the beginning of a new enterprise. After all, your business may be your livelihood now or in the future. It's your baby. It needs you constantly. You are nurturing it, building it. Without you, there is probably no one to answer the phone, talk with clients, deliver products, provide services, or whatever your business requires. You are your business and, if you aren't wise, your business could crumble.

Funds Low? Here's How to Go!

Here's a great way to approach the vacation situation when you're starting out in business, and even after you're a seasoned veterans: *Combine business with pleasure.*

Let's say you have the opportunity (or qualify) to go out of town for a business seminar or event, held in a great city or beautiful resort. Whether you're speaking or just attending, you may want to allow yourself a day or two, before or after the function, to enjoy the area.

For example, if the meeting is in Orlando, Florida, why not spend a day or two at Disney World, Sea World, Universal Studios or any of the other attractions? It would be great fun, and give you a reward for attending to your business—without spending any more money on travel expenses, and just a night or two more on food and lodging. You'll feel good taking a breather without jeopardizing your business!

We've done this a number of times, and always enjoy the time away without guilt. In fact, it offers the best of both worlds. You return home filled with motivation and refreshed as well. You'll feel good about what you're doing and where your life is headed. To top it off, you'll probably be able to write off the business portion of the trip as a business expense. Check with your accountant or tax preparer to be sure.

After eight years of having our own business, we now vacation just about whenever we want. We have been on mission trips with our church that allowed no incoming or outgoing calls, although we did leave the e-mail address with our printer who was finishing a job for us. We have even vacationed in the wilderness for several days where there were no phones, faxes, or e-mails, and our business just kept going! And yours can do likewise.

So you're going away and no one can stop you. You deserve it because you've earned it, and your family is counting on you both! But what will happen while you're gone?

Prepare—Go—Return

You've probably heard the old adage—*"If you fail to plan, you plan to fail."* Nothing could be truer when taking time away from a home-based or family-run business. Be proactive in making sure you can take your trip and not have an "out of business" sign greeting you when you come back.

Here are some of the proactive steps we've taken before, during, and after vacations—once our business was solid—that you could possibly do as well:

Advance Notice

Prepare your clients, associates, suppliers and others involved in the operation of your business as far in advance as necessary. If a client calls with a project even a month away from our vacation, we tell them our schedule and make sure it will work for them. To my recollection, we have never had anyone refuse to place a project with us when they hear we'll be on vacation. To the contrary, if you're doing a good job, most will say "Good for you," or "That's great—we'll get it finished before you leave."

In some cases, clients have placed work with us that started before we left and carried over after we've returned. In those cases, communication is especially crucial. We create production schedules telling them exactly where the project will be while we're gone. In most cases, we are able to schedule *client approval time* or *legal review* or *prototyping* during those periods—processes where our involvement is not needed.

Here We Go!

A week before our trip, we call, fax, or e-mail our clients again to let them know our exact departure and return dates, and any other information that may help them while we're gone. Chuck always creates a fun fax form offering to send a postcard from one of the places we're going if the client will fill out an attached *coupon* and fax it back. Now the clients are a part of our away time in an unexpected (for them) and non-invasive (for us) way. At the same time, it allows us to *stay in front of them* even when we are not there!

If you're in a leadership position where your success depends on empowering others, always send them a postcard from where you are. Include an encouraging note to keep them excited about coming with you next time.

Sorry We Missed You

You may want to change your voice mail message during times away. If you plan to check messages, state so on your recording and return the calls as soon as you can. Since you probably have a home office, tailor your message so as not to inform unsolicited callers how long you will be away.

We're Back!

Within a week of your return, touch base with all your clients and associates. You may be surprised at how well things kept going while you were away and, of course, you'll feel renewed. And depending on the nature of your business, you may even have business associates or employees who have been bringing more associates on or creating new business in another way—*while you were away!*

When you're self-employed, you don't have to give up vacations. Just blend business with pleasure and keep it fun. It's part of the joy of having a business together!

Chapter 8

—♥—

You're Doing *What*?

Five Style Differences to Celebrate

It's Great to Be Different

You've heard it before, but it's worth repeating: If everyone were exactly the same, life would be pretty boring.

It's true. Suppose everyone you know dressed exactly the same as you, ate the same things for lunch, liked the same professional sports teams, and had children who all looked and dressed alike? It might be kind of fun for a day or so. After that, though, we'd all be ready to go back to having some differences, wouldn't we?

Whether you've been married a month or 20 years, you can probably name dozens of ways you and your spouse are different in your likes, dislikes, fears, goals, and ambitions. But over the time you've been married, you've likely learned to adapt to most of those differences. Some you may have totally ignored while others were downplayed for the sake of marital bliss.

Here is a prediction, and you can cast it in stone:

When you begin working together, all of the ways that you are different—your various styles—will come out. Some may be welcomed, and some may be most unwelcome!

It will help you immeasurably to be aware of these style differences in the way you each do things as soon as you begin and as you continue building your business. In fact, it wouldn't hurt to start looking at your style differences before you make the move. But even if you have been in business for awhile together, it's never too late to begin appreciating and adapting to your differences.

Why? Because your personal style impacts everything you do—from how you dress to your work habits to how you interact with clients, prospects, vendors, or other business associates. When you bring those styles into your business in partnership with your spouse—the person who probably knows you better than anyone else on earth—they will sometimes seem larger than life. And because your livelihood may now be or perhaps will be tied to this venture, their importance can quickly be blown out of proportion.

By anticipating these styles differences, you can get over any initial surprise and get on with the business at hand. And believe us, there may be some surprising experiences when you see your spouse in action! (Especially if you've never worked together before.)

Chuck

I can still remember the telephone conversation Aprill had with the accounts payable manager at a large local advertising agency.

This agency has a reputation in the graphic arts community for paying its bills very slowly. And they had a bill from us that was more than 90 days past due.

It had always been my policy, when I ran the business by myself, to be somewhat low-key in collecting invoices. My logic was that being a one-person business, I had to interact with everyone in my client's organizations. It didn't make sense to blast people in other departments while being very nice to my primary contact. Besides, honey always works better than vinegar in interpersonal relationships. Follow the "platinum rule"—treat others as they want to be treated.

But, my taking this approach had also caused some of my clients to take advantage of my loose collection practices. So one of the things I asked Aprill to do when we transferred the financial responsibilities to her was be a little tougher on collections. The traditional interaction of accounts payable and accounts receivable staffs is probably, in many cases, best defined as thinly disguised contempt. But as long as I wasn't the person required to do the pushing, I didn't mind at least some pushing going on. Of the four Fs of effective personal interaction—firm, frank, friendly, and fair—I had flunked the "firm test." A marshmallow more closely represented my degree of firmness!

But then I heard Aprill do the pushing. She was tough— *really* tough! She told the person on the phone that this invoice had to be paid or that work in progress might stop until it was paid. And to top it off, did I mention this was our largest client at the time?

When she hung up the phone, I approached her about how I viewed her style as being, as delicately as I could put it, wrong! As I went on, I could see on her face the same thinly disguised contempt she had had for the accounts payable person. Then, she calmly reminded me that what she had done was what we already had agreed needed to be done. She reminded me that unpaid bills cost us money, and that we pay all of our bills on time and expect our clients to do the same.

She was right on all counts. Still, I walked away realizing that the simplest differences in style and technique for some may very well be the most challenging things to deal with and overcome when working with your spouse.

So, keep open clear lines of communication between you at all times so you can work through these things most efficiently and effectively. The key is to understand your spouse's intention and share how you feel. After that, their styles and techniques are easier to accept because they may make more sense to you.

Five Differences to Celebrate

After eight years, it's still not always easy to define, recognize, respect and deal with the different styles the two of us have. We're still working on it. Sometimes they become amazingly evident in our business pursuits.

But as we've worked together, and watched other couples we know who work together, we've come up with five basic style differences. And we've developed some suggestions on how husbands and wives who work together can celebrate them instead of agonize over them.

Difference #1—*Routine vs. Spontaneous*

One of you probably likes to *stay on track*, or *hold tight to the schedule.* You are probably a pro at prioritizing, a very efficient worker, and nothing gives you more joy than the completion of a task and being able to move on to the next task on your priority list.

The other one of you probably likes to accomplish things too. However, it's not quite so important to that person to keep the train chugging down the appointed track. If a better idea comes to them, they have no problem shifting gears, being flexible, and changing to a different course. When that person makes the changes, the other partner looks wounded and confused because they had not planned the day to include this new course of action. Now, *everything is ruined* and they will have to start all over. They will eventually get the train chugging down the track again—a different track, but on the right track in their estimation, nonetheless.

Prescription for husband-and-wife team success: When you are in business, there is a need for both routine and spontaneity. Most everyone has some measure of both, but one spouse is probably more routinized than the other and visa versa. Decide who is responsible for what, considering those strengths. If one person is more spontaneous in thought, let him or her set the short-, medium-, and long-term goals for you both to review and discuss. If the other is more into routine, let him or her create your filing system. There is nothing right or wrong about either—they are just different. So maximize your benefit as much as possible from those differences.

Difference #2—*Tune-Out vs. Leave Me Alone*

The TV is blasting, the microwave is beeping, and the children are screaming. Somehow your spouse, who is deep in thought, doesn't seem to hear anything. You don't understand how they can acknowledge your conversation—then twenty minutes later have no idea what you said. They are pouring over papers they dragged home from their all-too-consuming job. Most *normal* people (like you!) need peace, quiet, and a specified time set aside to focus—in order to think or work that hard on anything. How they can do it with all the noise is beyond your comprehension.

This trait and others will also show up as you do your business together. One of you, deep in paperwork, may not remember anything the other one said during that time. It's no problem to agree or disagree on something simple while barely breaking your chain of thought on your paperwork. Of course, you may not remember what you agreed to, but it was a simple question, and you trust your business partner knows what it is anyway.

Now if it's something of great consequence, you can probably discuss it a bit later. Nonetheless, your spouse has difficulty understanding why you sometimes need a specific time of quiet and concentration set aside to get some *real work* done. They think to themselves that they can get things done regardless of what noise and other distractions surround them. It just doesn't bother them and they don't understand why it bothers you.

Prescription for husband-and-wife team success: Take a few evenings and watch each other at home. Become a "fly on the wall" in your own home and observe what your spouse does when he or she is in total control of their activities. Don't make any suggestions, offer any alternatives, or bestow any requests. Just watch.

Does you spouse retreat to a quiet place and ask not to be disturbed? Or does he or she turn off the television and read, or keep it on and read? Does your mate turn everything off and take a nice, hot bath or shower? Or does he or she start a project that requires 47 tools and half of the family room to accomplish? How does your spouse use leisure time? This is probably indicative of what he or she will need to be productive as you work together, building your own business.

Make some notes: How long can your spouse comfortably go without initiating any conversation with you? How long can he or she sit still? Does your mate periodically interrupt what they are doing to start something else? Or are they focused; did they complete their current task first?

Just watch and remember. Then, when you see the same behavior as you work together, be understanding. This is who you married, and who you've decided to go into business with. You need to be patient, though, with the process of developing and maintaining this aspect of your relationship. And know that it can be the greatest thing in the world—incredibly worth the effort you invest in it!

Difference #3—*Direct vs. Diplomatic*

This style difference becomes very evident when working with clients and associates.

One of you, though polite and professional, doesn't *sugarcoat* (make more pleasant) information you are conveying to a client or associate—some appreciate the direct approach. They don't want to take the time or have the inclination to "tap dance" around your point. They need the information now to make a decision, and it works best for them when your communication is delivered in a straightforward manner.

When your partner hears you on the phone *telling it like it is*, they may be horrified. He or she might ask, "Can't you be more diplomatic and tactful?" You assert that a client or associate needs to be given every consideration and courtesy. This is especially true when it comes to delivering negative news, correcting a mistake, or discussing financial issues, like an overdue bill. You both agree totally that a client or associate needs to be given every consideration and courtesy, but your individual styles define what that means to you.

Prescription for husband-and-wife team success: The keys here are communication and standard business etiquette. Decide early what are appropriate ways to behave. Base these not only on your styles, but on how successful businesses operate.

Honesty and integrity will win over poor choices in style every day of the week. If you are honest but gruff, or if you have integrity but poor grammar, your potential for long-term success is much greater than if it were the other way around.

Do your best to be empathetic with others and consider how you would feel if you were on the receiving end of the communication. Is that person's style of communicating direct or diplomatic? Tune in on their level of reception, their style, and apologize if you say or do something they find offensive. Going and growing through challenges with a client, associate, or spouse, can be a real positive experience—bringing you to a new level in your relationship. Be kind and care about others as you go along.

Difference #4—*Macro vs. Micro*

We discussed these style differences a little in the finance chapter. One of you probably looks primarily at the day-to-day picture. It may be challenging for that person to project out more than a week. If this person goes beyond their comfort zone, they may panic. Yet, the other mate may find it unclear how the business can survive on the current information at hand.

One of you seems to worry very little, and is adept at projecting a successful future. He or she is a goal setter, and has either a mental picture or a written plan of the next five to ten years. It may be challenging for the other one of you to get past the end of the month. Yet, amazingly, when the two of you share your perspectives with each other, the picture looks better than either of you originally thought.

Prescription for husband-and-wife team success: Just as in the discussion of routine and spontaneous, successful businesses need those who can look at the big picture (macro) and those who can concentrate on the details (micro). It's essential to decide who is best at evaluating each decision, direction or priority. The spouse who is the macro-thinker is not the best one to make purchasing decisions. He or she will always *need* to buy a new computer or have *every* software upgrade available.

The spouse who is the micro-thinker is not the ideal one to decide on your sales strategy. He or she may *decide* it's in the best interest of your company to pursue a client who is making a $500 purchase in the next 7 days instead of focusing on the client who will be making a $25,000 purchase in the next 3 months. Long-term (macro) thinking is key in this instance.

Difference #5—*Deliberate vs. Head-On*

A situation arises that you need to attend to now. You already have the necessary details. However, you need to give it some thought and resolve whatever challenges it has presented. Therefore, you or your spouse need to devote some quality time to it. You or they need to sleep on it, deliberate, write down and weigh the pros and cons. You'll both need to talk about it together or with someone else who can help you.

The one of you (the macro-thinker) who isn't involved much or at all may wonder "*WHAT'S the big deal?* We've got all the information we need. Let's make the decision, get it done, and have a good night's sleep." To this person, whose approach is head-on, indecision is the worst decision. They probably believe it is always best to go with your gut, make the call(s), and deal with the consequences, which usually aren't that bad, after all.

Prescription for husband-and-wife team success: Learn what is truly urgent and what is important. (Hint: they are not always the same!) Ask yourself, "Can this wait until I'm finished with _____?" Or, "Is the only reason this seems urgent or important because someone else failed to do what they agreed to do on a timely basis? How will they ever learn if I jump every time they do this?"

Contemplate all major decisions, but make them and go on. Only analyze extensively when you absolutely need to. (Over-analysis can lead to "paralysis of analysis" which some people do deliberately or even unconsciously to delay taking action!) Respect your spouse if he or she is having a tough time getting over any hurdle. What may seem simple to you may be very complex to someone else. Why? Because we're all different, that's why!

These are just a few style differences we have noticed in each other as we work together and in our personal relationship. There are undoubtedly others.

As you build your business, if your partner has a style that bothers you, talk about it. Be fair, kind and forgiving about it, and be flexible, open-minded, and ready to acknowledge your own quirky style attributes. Your partner is likely to counterpoint, pointing out some things you do that you may not even be aware of. Just know that you can change some behaviors that aren't serving anyone. You will both probably want to make some changes for the sake of your business and your marriage.

Some modifications will be easy. Your spouse can help you understand that your straightforward style doesn't work with a particular client, and how you can be more diplomatic the next time and not let your temper flare.

However, we are who we are. I am who I am, and you are who you are. We can learn from our mistakes and shape, sculpt, and refine our styles. But our styles aren't us—they are just a reflection of our thinking.

Balancing Differences

One of the great things about being different from your spouse is that there is so much to learn from better understanding and appreciating your own and his or her styles. It becomes obvious, whether we want to admit it or not, that our way of doing things is certainly not the only one!

Ideally, we can all fine-tune our styles so that we are even more effective and pleasant to associate with. Rather than using our style as an excuse, we can be more aware of it and modify and balance it to better accomplish the tasks at hand.

Let's continue to say you are blunt and your spouse is diplomatic. There may be times that you could be misunderstood if you don't express something negative tactfully. As mentioned, you could ask your spouse what he or she would say and learn from that for future reference as well. Also, you could teach your spouse to have more directness and clarity in their communication. Perhaps they're so concerned about not offending people that their message gets lost in all the political correctness—it is so muted!

Working with your spouse and learning from and appreciating their styles can provide you with a wealth of knowledge of human nature—how to best work with (and live with!) them and how to be sensitive to and meet other's needs as you go along. You'll learn what is really important to discuss, and when to just say okay and let it go. Take a closer look at your differences and sort out what's really important to address—for the health of both your business and marriage. As a result, you can become a more rounded, flexible, and understanding person.

A Final Note on Ethics

You each may have nonnegotiable approaches that are not so much style as character. You refuse to take on a client's product because it does not promote a healthy lifestyle, even though it could be profitable for you. Or, a client of an associate in the same networking organization is in disagreement with the associate. Therefore, he wants to register with you rather than your associate to participate in your sales and marketing plan. You investigate to determine if the disagreement can be resolved between the client and your associate before you decide whether to register the client. Or maybe your spouse does not want to work with a particular client because he is in direct competition with an existing client. *These are not style issues.* Instead, they are character- or conscience-related situations based on ethics and moral principles. Recognize the difference, and approach them accordingly.

Respect your spouse's ethics and, while you may not totally agree right now, be prepared to discuss them and come to an agreement. After all, you would want to be in a partnership only where your personal values are upheld even if your own character is challenged in the process, right?

So celebrate! Who you are as individuals and as a team, and how you relate and respond to others, will largely determine how successful you are. Your differences can be your greatest strengths when you understand, accept, grow from, and build on them.

Success is a journey, not an endpoint—and it requires you to constantly look at each other's styles and ethics and re-examine your own to be the best you can be. But it sure beats having that *new manager's* ethics (if he or she has any!) and style at work as the only acceptable way of operating in the office, doesn't it? With your own business, you have so much more control than you do in a job, where you may be asked to do things you disagree with either ethically or stylewise.

Chapter 9

---❤---

Sorry, Honey— I've Grown Very Fond of Eating

Getting Started with a Less-Than-Enthusiastic Spouse

The Spouse Who Wants to Have a Marriage-Based Business Needs to Take the Lead

Overcoming objections others place in front of the two of you is one thing. However, overcoming objections one spouse places in front of the other is quite another.

The great news is, even if you both don't agree about working together, one of you can still get started. Whichever one of you who is enthusiastic about the idea can take the lead.

Benjamin Disraeli summed it up best when he wrote— "My idea of an agreeable person is the person who agrees with me."

In all relationships, including marriages, there are disagreements—expressed or unexpressed. We may disagree on the little things—what to have for dinner, which movie to see, or who to invite for Sunday lunch. We may disagree on the big things—which house to buy, whether or not to have children and, if so, how many, or what religion to follow. And we may disagree on hundreds of things in between.

Why is it so surprising, then, that so many couples are divided on the idea of working together?

For us, this wasn't a challenge. We had known for a long time that we wanted to have and build our own business. It was something we talked about, dreamed about, planned for and, when the time came, were ready to tackle. In fact, our main obstacles were in deciding what kind of business we wanted, and our own impatience in needing to wait until we had sufficiently paid our dues and gained the experience to know how to do it.

In short, we had a shared objective—we wanted to own our own business so that we could build our own empire, make our own decisions, set our own schedule, chart our own courses for our lives, and spend as much of our days together as possible.

Successful enterprises of all types, whether businesses, churches or civic organizations, are composed of individuals united in a common cause. They have shared objectives they are striving to achieve. Businesses band people together to create and sell products or provide services in order to make a profit. And, in some cases, like direct sales and franchising, also to share their free-enterprise opportunity with others. Churches and synagogues are groups of people who share the purpose of communicating spiritual or religious ideals and supporting others. Civic organizations can have any number of objectives, from political to environmental to humanitarian.

The challenge often is that most couples suffer from having no shared objectives. They start out with little more than a general idea of what a marriage needs to be, and they improvise from there. They know that most married couples have children, houses, cars, pets, jobs and churches or synagogues. But how someone pieces all of it together is a mystery they endeavor to learn through trial and error. The life stories of their marriages go something like this....

Couple A—*John and Susan*

John and Susan were married after dating three and a half years. John graduated with honors from the University of North Carolina with an MBA (Masters of Business Administration degree) in finance. Susan earned her BA (Bachelor of Arts degree) in political science from Duke University. After four years of marriage, while John was a rising star in the commercial lending division of a major national bank and Susan, an assistant director of a nonprofit political action committee, they had a son. Three years later, they had a daughter. Susan decided to become a stay-at-home mom, leaving the role of provider squarely on John.

As the children grew, so did John's responsibilities, as well as his time commitments at work. Fifty-, sixty-, even seventy-hour work weeks were not uncommon. All the while, Susan thrived in her role as a supermom. She spent her afternoons going between soccer practices and dance lessons, karate classes and swim meets. In the evenings, Susan had dinner with the children and kept a plate of food warm for John.

They thrived financially. By the time the children were in college, John was an executive vice president and Susan, who never went back to work full-time, was on the board of directors of three local steering committees. Their lives had been a success—except for the fact that they had lived them virtually apart. And although they had more than 25 years invested in each other, they couldn't figure out why they still felt personally unfulfilled—while in society's eyes they had it all.

Others don't fare so well. The statistics are staggering. Approximately 50 percent of all marriages fail. (This is a conservative estimate and it may vary, depending on what country you live in.) These couples often suffer from compounded problems. Detached spouses struggle with joint custody of children, alimony, child support payments, two residences—in essence, they lead fractured lives.

So not only do most couples have no shared objectives, but each individual within the couple has his or her own set of objectives. When two *individuals* marry and bring their *individual* objectives along, it's easy to understand how challenging it can be for them to build *shared* objectives.

Couple B—*George and Marilyn*

George was married with two teenage children and in his 40s when he first saw the sales and marketing plan presented by his friend Mack. His wife Marilyn, 32, was skeptical and refused to go with him, warning him, "Don't get any wild ideas about making a million dollars or sign anything while you're there."

Her reluctance was easy to understand. She was living comfortably and also seemed to enjoy her part-time job as a medical transcriptionist. George, on the other hand, although he was making a very good salary at his corporate job, felt he no longer had much control over his time. The boss demanded more and more dedication from him. In fact, it was becoming virtually impossible to even have a family dinner together because he had to work so late. But, he thought, how else was he going to climb the ladder of success?

Then Mack came along. A close friend since college, Mack shared with George how he and his wife Sue were building a sizable network of independent business owners across the nation. Mack always was good at making friends and now he was using that ability, along with Sue, to make more money.

George got excited about the possibilities of having his own business and working with Marilyn. So he registered himself to be a business owner in the network Mack and Sue so enthusiastically endorsed.

George was somewhat envious of Mack, who had Sue to work with him. Yet, even though Marilyn refused to register with him, George, still working his job, went on to build a successful business with the little free time he had. Marilyn, who was quite adept at finding ways to spend George's new-found secondary income, finally decided to join him after he retired from his job to do the business full-time!

Admittedly, it took a long while for Marilyn to warm up to the idea. But this fact has gotten her a lot of laughs as she shares her story with prospects, clients, and associates wherever she goes. She and George both teach that the spouse who wants to build a business with their reticent mate, needs to go ahead and do whatever it takes to do that—with or without the help of their spouse. Time and time again this has proven to be the key to attracting the reluctant spouse to join forces. In any endeavor, actually, this is true—whoever has the dream needs to follow through and not use the other person's objections or excuses as their own. As someone once said, "When the dream is big enough, the facts don't count."

Couple C—*Larry and Anne*

Anne and Larry met when they were both 16. It was love at first sight. They dated for almost a year. They married and moved into a one-bedroom apartment.

They had a baby girl, whom they named Amber. She came a little early but, fortunately, was healthy. Larry graduated from high school in May, and Anne got her diploma through a home study program introduced by her school district that same year.

Larry got a job as an air conditioning repair apprentice with a company owned by a family friend. The pay wasn't that great, but Larry felt it offered a future. Anne stayed at home with Amber for four months. Then, to help make ends meet, she went to work as a server at a restaurant on the 4 p.m. to 11 p.m. shift, four nights a week. Her mother kept Amber until Larry got off work—sometimes at 6 p.m., sometimes later.

For some reason, they were never able to get ahead financially. Larry worked hard, got his certification, and became lead man on the first shift. Anne moved on to bigger and better restaurants, sometimes making as much as $100 a night on tips alone. Still, the bill stack seemed to always be a little higher, while the bank account seemed a little lower every month.

Larry expressed serious concern to Anne that he didn't really know her and that she didn't really know him. He commented that they never spent any time together and had nothing in common but Amber. He admitted they were not the family he had expected. She shared his dismay at the situation they had gotten themselves into.

You, Too, Can Have Shared Objectives

Even couples with situations this challenging can have hope—They just need to establish shared objectives. And starting and building a business is one of the very *best* ways possible to *share* objectives—bar none!

But both spouses need to *want* to share objectives in order to do it successfully.

The great news is, at our cores, each of us wants essentially the same things. Although it may seem like we are each individuals seeking varied interests, we are all in search of some basic core needs, wants, and desires.

Maslow, a 20th century psychologist, first wrote about the fact that all people have the same basic needs. To this day, we want those basic needs fulfilled—food, water, clothing, and shelter.

You may agree that people of our time, especially in high-tech developed nations, see basic needs as givens. What used to be known as *wants* we have elevated to the level of *needs*—automobile and other transportation, television, computers, Internet access, fine foods, and the list goes on.

The fact is, after our basic needs are met, and we have a relatively comfortable existence, many of us spend the rest of our lives looking for such emotion-tied things as love, trust, acceptance, companionship, nurturing, and purpose. We have discovered that all the possessions in the world can't make up for a lack of these things in our lives.

Look at your marriage. You can find or develop these things in abundance in the relationship you have with your spouse. Depending on the state of your marriage, in repair or disrepair, this may or may not seem plausible to you. But be encouraged; contrary to what some may lead you to believe, working together is the best way to build that relationship! Here's why (along with another hidden truth)—*The more emotional the need, the more the fulfillment of that need relies on having shared objectives.*

Working together can enrich your married life, and here are some of the ways you are likely to notice:

Love and Trust Are Learned and Earned

You don't truly love someone the first time you meet him or her. You may be attracted to that person and even become instantly infatuated with them. But there is no such thing as *true* love at first sight. You *learn* to love people by first investing the time in learning about them and discovering their interests, wants, and needs. True, long-lasting trust is built over time. Talk is cheap, as they say.

What people actually do earns our trust or erodes it. And trusting someone at first glance can lead to disappointment. You learn to really trust people by observing how they act and react in life's situations, and how they treat you and others.

Learning and earning take time. As people change (which we all do) and grow (hopefully), we need to keep learning and earning every day. Working together gives you that time to invest in one another. You get the tremendous opportunity to get to know the *whole* person you married. You have the chance to experience all areas of their life—work, family, leisure, spiritual, financial, physical, mental, and social—in ways and in the depth that spouses who work apart simply can't!

Add any children you may have to the mix (in your business and personal lives), and you can begin to get a glimpse of the remarkable level of love and trust you can have by living your *entire* lives together. Observe other happy couples who work together building their own businesses and you'll sense the depth of satisfaction, joy, and fulfillment you can have as well.

Acceptance Is Built on Love

When you love someone, you come to accept that person—even with their unskilled and different behavior! Working together with your spouse tends to bring out all your qualities—desirable and not so desirable. You're likely to notice that both of you exercise very different personality traits in your entrepreneurial roles than you may have noticed in just living together.

Being with each other for a limited time each day, as most couples with jobs do, just doesn't enable you to grow your marriage like you could. Working together shows your strengths even more clearly, and also more obviously exposes your weaknesses. And when you work together as a couple, you have the opportunity to see all these things as you assume different roles. You may do this in your home-based business or outside your home environment—depending on how you are set up. The differences could also be apparent if you go out together and meet with potential or current clients or associates.

One of the best parts is, with the love and trust you and your spouse have learned and earned, *the acceptance you offer and receive from each other when you work together can enrich your marriage.* When you work through your challenges and celebrate your successes together, you'll probably experience love and acceptance at levels you may have never experienced before.

The Joy of Companionship Can Increase with the Number of Life Experiences You Share

Did you ever hit a hole-in-one when you were playing a round of golf by yourself and wish that your husband or wife had been there to witness it? Have you ever been on a business trip and experienced a breathtaking sunset, only to wish that he or she were there with you to see it?

Most of us desire companionship. We want to share our life with someone special to us. For the majority, that someone is a spouse we want to have as our life-long companion.

Working together gives you not one, but a whole array of life experiences you and your spouse would not have the opportunity to share otherwise. Making your first sale, registering your first associate, signing your first long-term contract, or turning your first quarterly profit will be something you'll both remember. And your sharing it together can increase the level of companionship you already have.

Nurturing Is Best When It Is Give and Receive

As children, we all long to be nurtured. As parents, we (hopefully!) long to nurture. As spouses, we long *to* both nurture and to *be* nurtured. And working together will give you ample opportunities for both.

In some instances, one spouse will nurture the other as he or she patiently teaches them a new skill. In other cases, one spouse will nurture the other when he or she has some sort of setback. And in some cases, you will nurture each other through shared successes and setbacks.

Either way, you can find opportunities every day to give and receive nurturing from each other. And the act of nurturing can help you expand your relationship beautifully and very likely much beyond what it is now.

The Purpose of Your Family Will Become More Comprehensive

As your business becomes a part of your daily life together, you will feel a sense of purpose that might have never surfaced otherwise. The common cause you will experience among yourself, your spouse and perhaps your working children who join you can pervade every aspect of your lives.

Suddenly, you will find that, while you may have always worked toward the common end of providing for and sustaining your family as a unit, now you'll see it more clearly—how it all fits together. You will *personally see* the long hours each of you may put in, the careful considerations you both make, and the committed effort each of you brings to the table for a single purpose—to make your business a success. It will become more and more evident as you go along—that you truly are a purpose-driven cohesive team.

A Deeper Commitment

In short, working together in your own business will require you to have an even deeper commitment to your relationship with your spouse and to the even more conscientious role of family leadership.

And here's a not-so-hidden truth—*No risk, no reward.*

Invest your whole self into your marriage and your family, and build a business together. The personal rewards will be great—greater, in fact, than you could ever have imagined they would be! There's just nothing like it.

Chapter 10

———— ❤ ————

Little Karen's Quite a Salesperson!

Bringing Children Into Your Business

Give Your Children a Chance to Participate

Those of you with children can't help but think how they might be affected by your building a marriage-based business. Whether they are young and energetic, or teenaged and maybe moody, children are probably the biggest part of your lives together. Therefore, in any business plan you may have, you need to consider their place in your family, your business, and your future.

We've all heard stories about stores, factories, and farms operated with the help of the entire family and later taken over and run by generations of children—perpetuating an inheritance through many, many years. Names like Carnegie, Vanderbilt, and Rockefeller may come to mind. There's lots of money passed on and businesses built with it. Some people would call it *old money,* with the connotation that its origins are a mystery. But it's *no* mystery. Somewhere along the line someone worked diligently for it, and their spouses and children worked alongside them. And together they built an empire!

Chances are good that some of your own friends, neighbors, acquaintances, or perhaps even family members, may be operating businesses begun and taught by their own grandfathers and grandmothers. Hank's Hardware down the street may be owned by Hank III; and when you go there you may meet young Henry or Henrietta, the *owners-in-training* for the next generation. You even may already be an integral part of such a family. If not, you may have wondered how your life could've been different had you built a family business together. You certainly would have seen your parents more, and maybe, depending on your family, you would have seen more of your brothers and sisters too. And that doesn't even include the possible financial advantages your parents may have been able to offer you through passing along a successful family-owned and -operated business.

So, maybe part of the dream you and your spouse share goes something like this:

To start building a business that not only employs the two of us, but can include our children and their children for generations to come.

Why Bring Your Children Into Your Business?
There are many reasons for wanting to include your children in your business. And they probably aren't too different from what Andrew Carnegie must have wanted for his family.

First, you want to know what your children are doing in their spare time. Let's face it, raising children in our technological age is more about channeling their time into wholesome, productive activities than it is about finding something to occupy their time. There are plenty of activities, but many of them are neither productive nor wholesome. For example, much of the television programming now aimed at children teaches morality standards with which few parents agree.

Second, you want to teach them responsibility and give them a good, healthy work ethic. Someone once came up with a saying we love—*"The harder I work, the luckier I get."* Most of the time, regardless of what others may think, it isn't luck at all that makes people successful. It's hard (and smart) work and perseverance that make the difference. The annals of million-aires throughout the world are full of stories about how they've been broke and then became wealthy.

The historical accounts of people who have been married for 50 or more years are full of stories of hard times financially, emotional strains in their relationships, and many other per-sonal and business challenges. The key is that all were, first of all, willing to *work through* the hard times rather than throw up their hands, blame their situation or others, and quit. And the harder the times got, the harder they worked to overcome the challenges. Therefore, later on, they were able to enjoy the fruits of their patience and perseverance. It usually took them many years to become "overnight successes."

Third, you may want to build something for your children's future—not just something that will put food on the table, clothe them, or necessarily even pay their college tuition—but something to which they can dedicate their professional lives, if they want to do so.

It's important, though, to accept the reality that your chil-dren may want to do something different with their lives than be a part of the family business. Whether or not they choose to continue doing so as an adult, participating in the business when they're living at home with you can be a wonderful growth experience for them.

A friend of ours, with three teenage children, started a brokerage business from the basement of his house after his employer *downsized* him. This taught him the first hard les-son—the only way to offer his family financial stability was to make sure that *he* was in control of the decisions.

As the business grew and grew, his wife joined the company. A few years later, his daughter returned to the nest, learned the business, and also became a valuable addition to the company.

Now, much to their delight, his son, a college sophomore, spends summer vacations and school breaks learning and helping in the business.

Our friends couldn't be happier, and they feel the most significant thing they've accomplished is building a business that doesn't just support them, but provides for their children as well. It offers all of them career opportunities with *the-sky's-the-limit* possibilities they would be hard-pressed to find anywhere else. It's a blessing to get to work with each other and their children every day. And the whole family agrees with that!

When You Picture Your Future, Do You See Your Family Working Together in Your Business?

There is no better place than in a family-owned business to teach your children the values you want them to have outside the home environment you provide. As you and your spouse make the transformation from just being partners in *love* to also being partners in *business*, you can involve your children. And as you learn the risks and rewards of being self-employed, it will most likely seem like a natural progression to include your children in your business too. Furthermore, as you build your business together, you'll all have great opportunities to learn to work with each other in a professional, enjoyable, and even an exciting way.

When you include your children, one thing will happen quickly—you'll surely spend more one-on-one time with them. You'll also be able to more effectively teach them lessons about responsibility, treating others well, and monetary values, in ways you never could have otherwise done. And, giving them allowances can serve that purpose, but only to a limited degree. Basically, with an allowance, you give them money and they decide how to spend it or whether to save it. Even if they have chores to do to "earn" their allowance, nonetheless *you still give it* to them.

But when you and your spouse put your children to work *in* the business, it's a whole different world—an educational world of helping others, learning the work ethic, risk and reward, supply and demand, and earnings and losses. It's not about cleaning off the table after dinner every night. When they participate in the business, it becomes a *real* job. And isn't a *real* job often the ultimate goal in the life of a young high school or college graduate? And isn't it also true that most high school and college grads never have the golden opportunity to become a *real* entrepreneur in their own family business? That's where they can truly flower—and make their dreams and goals a reality. And if, for some reason, they choose not to, they may change their mind later. Regardless, they have a *choice* most adult children simply don't have.

It may take a while for your children to understand that it takes *you* eight to fourteen hours a day at work to earn *your* "allowance." And then, do they ever realize how you must use *your* allowance for things they take for granted, like food, clothing, and shelter? Probably not, but that's okay. They're just children. But children growing up with parents who have a business enter adulthood with distinct advantages over those who do not. Among other things, they learn how to make and handle money responsibly—which is so important in today's world. They'll also learn how much better it is to be an entrepreneur instead of a person with a paycheck mentality.

As with everything in your business, there are a couple of things you need to be aware of from the start. First, admittedly, it will take extra time and effort, and probably extra patience, to include your children. While the idea of *working* with mom and dad may seem like the greatest one they've ever heard, reality could soon set in that having responsibilities may not be as much fun as playing their video games—not at first anyway. Second, keeping them interested and challenged will be key as it is with any other employee. If their role is set and they're never allowed to evolve, stretch and grow, and assume more and different responsibilities, they may become disinterested, disheartened and, yes, maybe even disgruntled.

But the payoffs are clear for them and for you. There will be less and less daycare to deal with. We may sometimes forget that daycare could be as stressful on our children as it might be on us. You'll be less and less concerned about how much time your children seem to spend in front of the television, playing video and computer games, or surfing the Internet. And that's not to mention being able to offer your children what most parents never put themselves in the position to offer their children—a *real job* making *real money*.

A Family Business Can Be Enjoyable and Educational

Including your children in your business can be enjoyable, educational, ensuring, enlightening and economical. You're certain to have fun when you see your children tackle a task and complete it in their own, perhaps very unique, way.

Think of it like this: If you enjoyed watching the first time your children took a step, ate with a fork, tied their own shoes, or hit a baseball, you're surely going to enjoy watching the first time they make a sale, answer the phone, sort the mail, and send an e-mail!

Having your children join you in your business allows them more time to learn from you. And it almost goes without saying that the more they learn from you the less they'll learn from someone else—especially those who may not have their best interests at heart.

This is also true when you have your children do their homework in your home-based office or with you wherever your office may be located. You're working together on your own projects and solving your challenges side by side. This can help you build a closer bond, just by your being together more. By keeping your office or other business workspace door open when you're working and they're doing their homework, you may even notice your children investing more time in their school assignments.

Would you like some fresh ideas? Bring up a business situation you'd like help with—either at dinner after everyone has had a chance to share what happened with them that day, or in your office. Make it a game and discover who can come up with the most creative idea to help overcome the challenge you presented. You may not find your solution then and there, but what you learn may be useful. At a minimum, you and your family have had a chance to work together again and help stretch everyone's thinking with this brainstorming!

Involve Your Children at Levels Appropriate to Their Ages
Give your young children simple tasks to do like easy filing and stuffing envelopes. Perhaps you could arrange it so they can sit at your desk or workspace while they do these tasks as you talk with clients or associates on the phone. You're setting an example of how a businessperson operates while helping them grow their self-esteem because they're likely to feel important and needed.

The older children can help you with more sophisticated tasks. Treat them like a trainee who is learning your business. They can attend business-related seminars, training sessions, conventions, opportunity meetings, product or service demonstrations and fairs, and other get-togethers associated with your business. The more you involve them in these activities as greeters, snack preparers, or with other age appropriate tasks, the more they'll learn and develop their confidence. Be creative—it'll be worth it!

Set Aside Family Time
Be sure to devote some special time to your children when you are only doing personal things—not business-related things. For example, take them out to dinner. Focus solely on

them—turning off your cell phone and/or pager. Look at and listen to them, touch and hug them, and tell and show them you love and treasure them.

Schedule a family evening each week where you do something fun together. Pack a picnic and go to the park, go swimming, take a bike ride, go outside and play basketball, make some special treat in the kitchen, play a game, or just sit in the family room and talk.

Be sure you let your children know they are important to you as people—not just as an extra set of hands to work in your business. Family fun time can help you communicate this. It also brings some often much-needed balance to what may be your very busy life of working your job and building your business on the side as well as juggling family and other personal responsibilities.

Chuck

When I was growing up, my mom worked full-time as a music store manager. With my love of music, I couldn't imagine one of my parents working at a better place!

After school, I'd ride my bicycle to the store and generally just hang around. I'd play the instruments, listen to music, and probably get in the way more than anything.

I liked the music store so much that by the time I was 14, I wanted to start working there. At the time, there were no laws against employing a 14-year-old, so my mom put me to work right at the bottom of the ladder. I vacuumed, unloaded stock, and did just about anything that was needed. Sometimes, my compensation would be an album or a set of guitar strings rather than a paycheck. But, at 14, I didn't have the money to buy such things on my own anyway, so that was great.

I worked there throughout my high school years and during the summers of my college years. I didn't realize it at the time, but I was learning a lot about business and life while working at my mother's side.

I don't ever remember Mom closing early, or opening late—regardless of how much she sometimes wanted to. She never missed a day of work from a *fake* sick day, and I remember her missing very few *real* sick days. She made bank deposits daily to keep the cash flowing. Mom always gave customers the benefit of the doubt, and she enjoyed a lot of loyalty because she offered a high level of service.

I know how hard my father worked since he was always self-employed from the age of 25. Although I now have a special appreciation for him, I actually *saw* how hard my mother worked. So it was natural that her work ethic became my model. I learned about business and what it means to work diligently day in and day out from my mother.

One thing never occurred to me until I was grown and well into my own career. My mom employing me and having me work with her gave her a sure-fire way to keep me out of trouble! Fortunately, I wasn't a child who had tendencies to get into a lot of trouble anyway. But if I had been that way it certainly would have been much harder to get into mischief considering the amount of time I spent with her.

Spending lots of time together was the key. She had to work to make ends meet. But ingeniously, she found a way to parent me while she worked. It was a truly remarkable experience!

Ensuring and Enlightening

It isn't just your children who will benefit from working by your side. You'll benefit from working with them too! One way will simply be the *peace of mind* you'll have.

When you and your spouse work together and have your children working with you, you'll know exactly where they are, what they're involved in, and what they're likely to be learning. Most importantly, you'll know exactly who has the most influence in shaping their lives—*the two of you!*

It takes an investment of time to build and run your business, and even more time to include your children. Rest assured, though, that it will be time well invested. For example, chances are excellent you'll learn how to be an even better parent when you see them in action and interact with them as you work together. Because you've taken the initiative to build a family business and include your children, you'll share experiences you would not otherwise have had.

Again, allowing children to participate with you in your business will stretch them in ways they wouldn't be stretched just being at home, doing ordinary household jobs. You'll be able to offer them opportunities, challenges, and responsibilities far different than what they'd experience just doing household chores. (However, they need to help with household chores too!)

As you work with them and watch them accomplish more and more, you'll be able to observe firsthand as your child uses his or her own personal strengths, talents, and abilities to get a job done. You'll also have additional opportunities to help them maximize their strengths and minimize their weaknesses as you prepare them for adult life. Where you invest your personal time *at home* teaching them the mechanics of life, you can also invest your business-related time *at work* in your company, teaching them the necessities of both earning a living and creating a fine lifestyle. This will be an experience you are only likely to have while building a business together as husband and wife, and including your children in the mix.

Chances are also excellent that, even if your children's talents and interests don't mirror your own, you'll still be able to use their strengths somewhere, somehow, to enhance your business. (This alone can be a tremendous self-esteem builder for your children.) You're likely to feel such a remarkable sense of accomplishment because your family is pulling together in joint efforts toward your goals and dreams. The satisfaction and joy you're likely to have from this experience will be surpassed by very few other things you could ever do as parents.

Aprill

My father was production manager at our hometown newspaper. When I was a teenager, he decided to put me to work part-time at the composition table. And although we had a great relationship and there was nothing I wanted more than to do a good job, it simply wasn't the kind of job at which I could excel.

After a few tearful, frustrating days, I told my father what I *really* wanted to do was to write articles for the newspaper. However, at the time, there was no part-time job in the editorial department for an inexperienced teenaged writer. But, fortunately, as time went on, I did get some exciting opportunities to write a few feature articles complete with photos and bylines. No matter what other chance would have presented itself, I couldn't have been happier at that point in my life.

Most importantly, my father and I learned that our talents and strengths did not have to be identical to share an interest in the same business.

Economical

Finally, the work your children do in the business may also save you both time and money. In some instances, their participation can *make* money for the business. And having your children as employees may also offer some tax advantages to the business and ultimately to you, depending on how your business is structured.

Some friends of ours, who are also suppliers, own a commercial photography studio. The business employs the husband, wife, and their son and daughter, ages ten and seven. The husband is the principal photographer and the primary point person in managing and interacting with their clients. The wife is a food stylist, organizes props for the photo shoots, and manages the books and finances. The children are in the studio three or four afternoons each week.

After completing their homework assignments at a work area the couple has created just for them, the children have responsibilities that relate to the business. As you might expect, they do a lot of the simple chores—emptying trash, sweeping floors, and dusting equipment.

As a bonus, having the children around gives the studio an added capability needed from time to time by select clients—child models! Available at a reduced rate (compared to professional modeling agencies), photos of the children have appeared in annual reports, catalogs, corporate brochures and a variety of advertising materials. The industries which have benefited from this convenience and cost-effective idea have ranged from food companies to outdoor power equipment manufacturers and home improvement contractors.

Because their company is structured as a corporation (which may not be recommended for you—check with your leader, mentor, accountant, or other advisor), our friends are able to pay the children up to the legal limit, allowing the parents to shelter some of the company's earnings from taxes. The children are taught to save 75 percent of their earnings, and their allowances have been eliminated and replaced by their earned income.

The results? The children give more consideration to their personal purchases and have an enhanced appreciation for the value of money. They also understand investing and its benefits. And, to top it off, the children have a growing investment portfolio that, in eight to twelve years, will more than pay for their college educations at any institutions they may choose to attend.

Your children don't have to have an interest specifically in the core capabilities of your business to make a valuable contribution. For example, let's say you have a teenager or college student who is an Internet enthusiast and you have an e-commerce-based distribution business. He or she could encourage others to register with your company to purchase their products and services, and to share the opportunity with others. If your son or daughter is a computer whiz and you have a retail store, he or she might be able to move your business to the web at a fraction of the cost of a professional designer. If successful, their efforts might evolve into a side business offering web page design services.

Your business may be photography (like our friends) but your teenager may have aspirations in film. You could choose to expand your business to include videography and invite them on-board. Encourage your children to express themselves in some manner through your business, and it's highly likely you'll all grow and learn in ways you never imagined!

It's Never Too Early

If your children are too young to actually be of help, you can pique their interest now. Then, when they're old enough, they may be eager to begin being a part of things. Say you have several products available through your business. Show them these products one by one, and explain how they work and what makes them special. This is also a good way to practice your presentation skills!

Give them empty product containers (if they are safe) to play with, and help them create their own pretend *store*. Explain that if you sell so much of the products, then in a few months the family can go to an amusement park or take a vacation. You will find their enthusiasm over your business and products motivational and contagious. Their presence and perspective will shed a whole new light on your enterprise!

If you sell a service, show them what you do and how you do it. They may not understand something as complicated as a computer design program, but they'll understand a computer scan of a picture of themselves with a funny hat. If you draw house plans, show them how you do it, start to finish. And be sure to include some kind of building toys in their toy collection.

If you are an accountant, show them a completed tax return. Explain that because you filled out the form exactly right and helped the clients save money, the clients will now be able to buy their own children a jungle gym. Well, you get the picture. Find a way that is age-appropriate to involve even the youngest members of your family, as soon as you can reasonably do so.

As the children get older, you can easily involve them in order fulfillment, office maintenance, filing, paper shredding, phone answering, and other things, depending on the nature of your business and their skills and inclinations. Of course, they're likely to expect to earn some money for their services, but what better way to teach commerce and business to your children than by compensating them for their contributions to your own business! And, they'll truly deserve to be paid. They are part of the business now, just as you had envisioned.

Don and Deana

Don and Deana were hesitant to include their children, ages eight and thirteen, in their skin care product business. The eight-year-old, Scott, with his endless energy and questions, could be quite distracting. Karen, the petite, just-turned-teenager, was, let's say, going through some adolescent challenges. But as the business grew, requiring more of Deana's time, she and Don chose to give the children afternoon duties in the house as well as in the business.

They created a list of products to be included in the sales kits, and it was Scott's job to check and replenish the kits after every sales call. He also emptied office trash cans, dusted, and ran the vacuum. Deana spent some time with Karen and taught her how to answer the business phone in a professional manner, as well as how the filing system was organized. But the most pleasant surprise came when little Karen, on her own initiative, started selling products to her friends and their parents! Don and Deana soon realized this was a very natural path for a young girl and her friends who were suddenly interested in their appearance and ways to make it better.

Now the family needed to discuss how the children would be paid for their work, particularly Karen. Within a few months, some of her friends' parents had also started sharing and selling the products, giving Karen a very important role in helping to build the family business. Don and Deana decided that Karen could keep a certain percentage of her earnings for spending, with the remaining amount to be invested toward her college education.

The most exciting part was that Karen would be able to keep making the business work for her through college and beyond. There would be no need for her to get a part-time job, which might have required her to have a car on campus or keep late hours. She could do her schoolwork, keep sharing and promoting the products, and still have time to enjoy everything else college life offered.

Six years later, with Karen away at school, Don and Deana began to help Scott find more important roles in the business. This helped them fund his college education and provide him with experiences that could give him greater advantages further down the road.

A few years later, they were amazed at how their family had accomplished so much with so little. It may have been small in monetary terms but, in the bigger scheme of things, was it *really* so little? No, absolutely not, they decided. The biggest factor in their success, Don and Deana realized, had been making that success happen as a family! Everyone pitched in, and it all worked out beautifully with lots of love and attention for the children, who blossomed into fine, happy adults as a result. It was now hard to believe they ever had any doubts! They observed that if only other families would work together like they did, they would experience more happiness and joy, as well as success.

Chapter 11

---**w**---

Home Sweet Office—
Office Sweet Home

To Work at Home, or To Live at Work?
That Is the Question

Where Do You Really Want to Be?

Are you one of those people who fights rush hour traffic to and from your stressful job? Has it been quite a long time now since you first yearned to work at home? Is the home-to-work/work-to-home grind getting to you?

Perhaps you're a wife and mother who would like to continue your career and work from home—completing everything you now accomplish at the office while your babies are sleeping and/or your children are at school. You'd be able to put a pot of soup on the stove and have laundry going—all while you're doing the work you get paid for. You could show up at the office once a week, or better yet, receive e-mail, faxes, or overnight packages of the things you need to do your job—and still be able to do what the company needs you to do.

You could work in your sweat pants if you want, with no makeup and certainly no pantyhose. If neighbors started stopping by for mid-morning coffee, well, after the first time, you would need to be firm about having your job to do. And if you got a cold, you wouldn't feel you had to go in and feel miserable and possibly infect a whole office. You could simply slouch over the work in your home office which may, at first, be in a closet-sized space bedroom! Better yet, you could just lie down and rest for a few minutes, and then get up and go back at it.

Yes, it's a dream for many women *and* men to work at home. (And, even though some companies are encouraging certain employees to work from home as a more economical option—you're *still* not your own boss!) Thousands of couples make it happen for themselves and their families every day by operating a marriage-based business.

These people transitioned to wherever in their house they could set up an office—sometimes starting at the kitchen table. Some have discovered one of those really great kits that turn a closet or even an armoire into a compact office that can be closed and forgotten when the workday is over. Or perhaps they have closed-in, heated, painted, and partitioned their garage for a bigger office space. They may have looked at their over-sized great room and, with a strategically-placed sofa, sectioned it into a family area and office area. Some have transformed their cozy dens with built-in shelves and cabinets into really terrific office space. And, as you probably know, it's not just women doing it—it's both men and women who are excited about the convenient, comfortable lifestyle of working at home.

This major trend shows no signs of decreasing in the decades to come. As the twenty-first century is moving into full swing, more people are working from their homes than ever before.

You may be running your own independent home-based business, telecommuting with your existing employer, selling products or services as an independent representative or commissioned salesperson for a major corporation, or doing something else. Regardless of exactly what you've chosen to do or are contemplating doing, working at home can now be a viable alternative for you and your family as it is for more and more people all over the world.

Now let's take a look at why this is happening:

The Technological Leap

As late as 1985 many offices looked and functioned much as they had for the previous 50 years. Sure, there had been innovations, but most were mere upgrades to systems and equipment that had been employed for decades.

Typewriters were still the major means of producing business documents. In 1955 most typewriters were manual. And as Henry Ford had once said about his cars, "They came in any color, as long as it was black."

By 1985 typewriters were still around, but they had evolved. They were now sleek, electronic models capable of putting words on paper faster than most people could make their fingers move. They had self-correction capabilities with onboard correction tape and LCD line displays. Their operational features had evolved to include wonderful innovations like memory and a limited degree of programming capability.

But, alas, they were still typewriters.

In 1955 if you wanted nine copies of the finished document you were about to type, you had two choices. First, you could type it nine times (how exciting!). Second, you could load three sheets at a time and place a piece of carbon paper between each sheet. The copy under the first sheet of carbon would be fair; the copy under the second sheet would be poor.

By 1985 you could take your finished document, feed it into a photocopy machine and (as long as all you were copying was black words on white paper) get nine, ninety or nine hundred copies. And if you so desired, the photocopy machine could even collate and staple them too!

Now that you have your document completed, how about delivery?

In 1955 you had a couple of options. First, if you needed to take it across town, you or someone in your office could drive it there—assuming you had a car, which was not a foregone conclusion in 1955! If you wanted to send it across the country, you had to use the mail system. Depending on the class you sent it, it might arrive in three days, or two weeks. (It's worth noting that the fastest delivery—air mail—still used prop planes. And that was after it was delivered to an air field, which might be two or more days away.)

Fast forward to 1985. If you worked in a major metropolitan area and wanted to send your document to another major metropolitan area, you could now use any of several overnight delivery services. Your package would be picked up at your door and delivered the next day. If you were sending it to a rural location, it might take two days. But, still, you were guaranteed delivery in as little as two days.

Today, you don't have to look as far back as 1955 to say, "How did we ever do business that way?" You only need to think back to 1985 to say it!

The technological advances in communication and information transfer since 1985 have been more immense than during any other period of human history.

Tomorrow, look around your office and see if you can find a typewriter. Go from office to office and floor to floor. Ask. If there is one, there is probably only one, and it is likely used to handle some rather archaic function that is equally out-of-date.

Overnight delivery is still widely used. And even the U.S. Postal Service offers it. The difference? It is not only available to any address in the U.S., but to most addresses worldwide. Worldwide! (Perhaps in whatever country you may live in outside the U.S., you have such worldwide and handy service readily available too.)

Don't want to wait? Fax it! I remember the first fax machine I ever saw. It was in 1986 and it ran at a rate of about 15 minutes per page. (That's not 15 pages per minute—*15 min-*

utes per page!) Today? Plain paper fax machines can even transmit pages not only in seconds, but also in beautiful color! Need it even faster? Use e-mail. Most businesses have access to the Internet, and through that access they use e-mail to communicate regularly with internal and external sources. And we won't even take the time to go into how the use of the World Wide Web, videoconferencing, digital telephones and pagers, and high-capacity computer-storage media have revolutionized the way most of us do business.

Understandably, companies are finding it easier in many ways to have employees work from virtual offices in their homes than to have them centrally located. The idea of working from home has gained tremendous popularity and respect. Costs are many times lower, and employee satisfaction is considerably higher. Productivity is generally better, and employee retention rates go up.

"So why doesn't *everyone* work from home?" you may be asking.

Home-Based Business—The Dream of Many

There is no question that working from home can add a measure of quality to your daily life. No more stressful commuting during rush hour in all kinds of weather conditions. No more spending after-tax income on expensive wardrobes. And no more rushing out the door before your children are off to school. In fact, you're even there to greet them when they get home from school!

When we started our business, we were aware that many couples ran their own business out of a spare bedroom. More and more people who worked for larger companies, and even some who worked for small companies, had begun using home offices. And, of course, salespeople throughout the years had based themselves at home and had run successful careers without ever going into an office.

And, it certainly is the most inexpensive route.

So that's what we did. With Chuck being the only employee, it made sense to convert a spare, unused bedroom into a fully-equipped office with computer, printer, fax machine, two-line telephone, office lighting, and professional decor. Cost (not including equipment that could ultimately be used regardless of where the office may eventually be located): $200.

Chuck

When we started our business, I had just come out of what I would consider the typical rat-race environment. I had been vice president of an advertising agency of about 60 people, nestled inside a $100 million corporation. The two departments I had responsibility for included about half of the 60 people in the company. I was in charge of the day-to-day management and, in addition, had primary sales responsibilities for about $3 million worth of new business.

The days were long, many times 14 hours. An advertising agency generally has two types of people. First, there are the creative people. They are more expressive, visual, verbal and, with that, more fragile in ego and require more nurturing. Then there are the account people. They are more assertive, numbers- and goals-oriented, hard driving and more direct, and require a challenge.

And I managed a department of each!

Needless to say, much of my day was spent just doing my level best to survive. I spent a lot of time massaging emotions on both sides. Another chunk of time was spent doing what I do worst—corporate management. Finally, a small chunk of time was left over to do what I do best—create and execute advertising ideas for clients.

I came home every day exhausted, wondering whether or not I had accomplished anything. So the idea of working in my house was very appealing. And, as I started working from home, I thought I had landed in heaven.

I set up the business in May. It was the best part of spring. For the first three months, I couldn't believe how good it was to get up, go into the office in a pair of shorts and a T-shirt, and start doing business. If I had to meet a client, I got dressed and met them, returned home and changed back into my shorts. I ate a long lunch on the deck, walked the dog whenever I felt like it, and had dinner ready when Aprill got home. It was great!

When most people consider working at home, they may say, *"Oh, I don't know how you get motivated to get up and going."* My challenge was just the opposite. I never stopped. I worked all day. My long lunches, breaks, and dog walks soon ceased. I worked, ate dinner, and worked some more. I came home from anywhere we went, checked my fax machine and phone messages, and if there was anything to act on, I did it then—whether it was 8 p.m. or 11 p.m.

So, the caution here is to create boundaries for yourself. Be sure you incorporate personal time with your spouse and family. You'll just wear yourself out if you work all the time. Discuss this with your spouse and reach an agreement about how you'll operate your business and family life to maximize both. Set aside a day of rest and rejuvenation, each week if possible—or at least several hours. As we discussed before, create a family night. Get out of the house and do something different. Balance as much as possible.

Aprill
Like a lot of women, it had been my dream to work from home. It would be just wonderful to have a career that *could* thrive with only a desk in a corner of the family room. So as I joined the business with Chuck, I was eager to work at home in a spare bedroom converted to an office. But there were all kinds of distractions—all the other jobs that were calling for me as I secluded myself upstairs. Even with the entire house quiet, I could still hear the refrigerator asking me to come down and figure out what we'd have for dinner.

People who work at home need to be focused, not allow themselves to be distracted by every little noise or activity in the house, and they need to be serious about their work. Fortunately, those working at home do not generally expect a large number of people in and out due to their business. They generally don't have a storefront. Such dedicated people, if engrossed in an important phone call or under deadline pressure, do not hear the dog barking like crazy and then get up to see what is going on.

People who aren't focused often stop what they're doing to check things out. They may hear something in the backyard, find some baby birds have fallen out of their nest, and the mother bird is trying to distract the dog. That person finally finds their shoes, puts them on, runs outside and wrestles the dog into the house. Then, he or she finds the scattered birds and their nest, looks around for a safe place, gets the ladder out of the garage, tries out several ledges, places the nest on one and puts away the ladder. Finally, he or she goes back in, looks out, doesn't see the mother coming back, gets the ladder back out, gets the nest and puts it back where it was found on the ground, puts the ladder away, comes back in, tells the dog to hush about a thousand times, and notices it's time to start dinner.

Some people need to work harder at disciplining themselves to stay in their home office and focus on their business. They need to learn to ignore things happening around the house that seem to demand immediate attention. They learn to let these things go rather than giving non-business-related chores priority, figuring they'll get this little stuff done before they get down to real work. That thinking can quickly take you off-track. Things going on around the house can be interesting and distracting—if you don't watch out. My usual style is *tune-out*, but I can turn that button on and off at will.

Sometimes I like to work ahead. If I can get a casserole assembled on my lunch break, I am that far ahead of the dinner rush. Of course, an hour of productivity in the office is still lost, although it doesn't seem that way. It's a matter of adhering to your highest priorities, each and every day.

You can perform at an optimal level with a professional, confident attitude at home even though it may take conscious self-talk at first to get yourself to switch gears. You'll be going from just relaxing and doing household or outside chores at home to running your business and all its attendant activities from home. You can do it—many people have.

You May Need More Space—A Decently-Sized, Designated Area Where You Can *Both* Fit in and Work Comfortably

Some friends of ours (a married couple) are both outside salespeople for two different companies. They both work from home, from the same small office which was converted from a bedroom. Both are superb salespeople, the kind who have natural exuberance in their voices when talking to a client, and both feel the need to always speak loudly and clearly. And when they are both on their separate business lines, closing a deal, making appointments and such, the din is deafening. Their cats even go downstairs to hide under the sofa. It doesn't bother either of them in the least, and evidently not their clients. In contrast, we dislike it if the radio is just a tiny bit too loud when we're making a business phone call.

Being together in a small area wouldn't work for us because Chuck simply needs a lot of space. He needs to spread out. Compactness is not a virtue in his work world. Some of the nay-sayers, (remember them?) may have asked you how you would be (or are) able to be relatively peacefully together all day. Well, adequately-designed office space helps you to be more happily productive together.

If you each work from home and both need your space, find a way to carve out separate office spaces for each of you, as small as they may be. Or maybe you'll choose to occupy the same office at different times. Be open-minded and flexible. If you are a little tight on space right now, maybe you can expand later. For example, when one of your children leaves home for college, you can expand into that room.

Exceptions to the Rule

In some cases, you may not be able to work out of your home because of the nature of your business. For example, if you have a franchise business, like a McDonald's, you definitely need another location! In some cases, if you have clients streaming in and out and you have a showroom, it may not be possible or practical to accommodate that in your neighborhood because of zoning or other practical reasons.

So, How Will You Set Up Your Business?

It's not as challenging as it may sound to decide what's best for you. The important thing is to look at *what your business requires*, and then how your individual styles fit into your plans, goals and visions for your business.

Does your business require a storefront, parking for employees and clients, and a sign? If you have your heart set on having such a business and are willing to work outside your home, you will probably need to start looking for space, even if one or both of you always dreamed of working from home. (Maybe you still can do *some* of the work at home, as long as you have appropriate people-coverage at your place of business.)

If you discover that you want to switch gears to the simplicity and low cost of working totally from home, you will need to build a different business—perhaps direct sales using e-commerce, or something else that doesn't require the potentially high overhead of an outside-the-home location. You could do this possibly on the side, until the income from your new business is enough to support itself and you and your family. Then you could sell your first business and work from home. (If your dream is to work totally from home, your best bet is to find a home-based business you like and build it—it'll save you time and money in the long-run!)

Do you basically just need one or two business phone lines, perhaps a computer and printer, a fax machine and maybe an empty closet for product inventory (like our sales friends)? Then you could probably operate from home.

Once you decide what your business requires, talk about what your *styles* require. You may both really want a separate office space but know that won't be feasible until the business is off and running, and you can afford to partition a large room at home. In that case, turn what you already have into the best work environment possible for the both of you and your children, as they participate more and more in your business.

For many businesses and the people who build and run them, the home office scenario is definitely the best. Business clients and vendors don't care where you are operating from, as long as you have a phone, fax, e-mail, and an Internet connection. If your business doesn't require commercial space, and you train (or retrain) yourself to work in a home office, you have probably just saved yourself a lot of money in rent.

Say you plan to run your business from your home. Go ahead and ask yourself the following questions about your style and the needs of your family:

What would you like your dream home office to be like? Visualize how you want it to be and make it happen as you can afford to do so. For example, say you are deeply in debt and right now wouldn't be a good time to buy a new desk. Use your kitchen table! Then, when you have a little extra cash, shop the classified ads for a used desk.

Talk to your leader, mentor, or other advisor about how to set up your home office—so you can be successful. Be open and honest with them about your financial situation so they can counsel you how best to invest your money into your business. Find out what tools and supplies you need, what educational/motivational audio and video tapes, brochures, CDs, and books they may recommend, what training sessions, seminars, and conventions to attend, and other learning opportunities that are available. And ask them if there's anything else you need to run your home-based business successfully.

Ask for help on training yourself to have the self-discipline it takes to be focused on your business priorities, and to set boundaries that work for you and your family. You *can* make your home office a success. You can do exactly what you need to do to juggle at-home and at-work responsibilities and make your business grow and prosper.

Do you need to have a home office so that you can keep your children out of daycare? Does your family need you to make a home office work for your business? If so, you may choose to buckle down and figure out how to make it work, even if it requires leaving your comfort zone of home-to-work/work-to-home habits.

You certainly have a lot to think about. But to get a change in results requires a change in habits. You need to be patient with yourself as you transition to working at home. You'll discover how you and your family can work the most effectively and enjoyably together. Look at it as a creative adventure. Celebrate every step of this positive change and share what you are learning with others who also want to get out of their daily grind and work from home.

In fact, go share this book with them. It could really help.

Chapter 12

—♥—

The Payoffs of Working Together

We Never Imagined Our Marriage Could Be So Wonderful

Some of the Advantages of Operating a Marriage-Based Business

We've discussed many of the great payoffs you can have when you work with your spouse (and your family)—11 chapters' worth! You may have a favorite, such as having a more flexible schedule and the freedom to control it; earning money that, once the business expenses are paid, goes directly to you and your family and no one else; or creating a life and career together that could not be duplicated separately. They're all excellent payoffs, don't you agree?

In light of all the previous, heavier discussions, we've decided to close with a list of *quick-hit reasons* you will enjoy working with your spouse. We feel certain that after the first year, you'll have many of your own thoughts to add to this list.

Here are ours. Enjoy!

♥ You can kiss each other anytime you want.

♥ You aren't doing anything wrong by sleeping with your business partner.

♥ You don't have to be embarrassed if you stay in the "company" bathroom a long time.

♥ You can take a sick day without keeping track of how many you have left.

♥ You can talk about what you want (or where to go) for dinner while working on business.

♥ If you take a long lunch to shop around Christmas, Hanukkah, or a birthday or wedding, no one gives you a dirty look when you get back.

♥ If you need a hug, you can ask for it and get one.

♥ If you *really* need a hug, you probably don't have to even ask for one!

♥ You don't have to be embarrassed if you are having digestive challenges.

♥ You can call your doctor without the need for privacy.

♥ The coffee is made just the way you like it.

♥ You can talk to each other all day long.

♥ You can talk to each other all night long.

♥ You can talk to each other about home stuff during the day.

♥ You can talk to each other about business stuff during the night.

♥ You don't have to impress your co-workers with new clothes and shoes.

♥ You don't even have to wear shoes.

♥ You can take time off to work for charity because you both know it's a good thing.

♥ No one can take your parking space.

♥ You have no worries about whether the things on your desk or bulletin board are politically correct or could be considered sexual harassment.

♥ Your child(ren) can come into the office.

♥ Your pets can come into the office.

♥ If you are walking across the office and a song comes on the radio that makes you want to dance or sing, you can.

♥ If you want to listen to jazz and rock music in the same morning, you can.

♥ If your lunch is missing from the company refrigerator, it doesn't take a long time to figure out who took it.

♥ Since you've had breakfast together, you already know whether or not your co-worker may need an attitude adjustment that day.

♥ If you don't have a good picture of your spouse to go on your desk, it's okay.

♥ You can feel free to use the petty cash.

♥ You can wear shorts.

♥ You can wear briefs.

♥ You'll have no problem finding a place large enough to host your company holiday parties.

♥ If your chair is too uncomfortable to take a nap in, you can stretch out on the floor.

In short, building a business with your spouse (and family) could be the best thing you ever do in your life!

Chapter 13

———— ♥ ————

The Exciting Journey...
Home

Ready, Set, Go!

It's Time to Move On

If you haven't already done so, you need to start taking action, if you're truly serious about having your own marriage-based business. And, as with anything else, there are any number of ways to begin.

There are several factors that impact how you and your spouse will start your business. Almost all of them are tied to your answer to one single but important question:

How well are you prepared financially to fund your current lifestyle—your short-term and long-term financial obligations, and the start-up costs of your new fledgling company?

At first, most of us would have the same answer: We are not financially secure enough to quit our jobs and live without an income while we work to build a profitable business. Statistics would agree. Most of us need to keep our "day jobs." In fact, even if you're able to just let go of one or both of your jobs, it may be wiser not to do so and rather, build your business on the side until you are in a more solid financial position. Your mentor, leader, or advisor can guide you on this one.

For most families, the majority of their income goes to fund their lifestyle. Are you part of this group? Regardless of your tax bracket, do you spend most of your total income on paying for your home, car(s), food, utilities, other household and personal necessities, hobbies, entertainment and education? All of those items and others constitute your current lifestyle. Unless you're independently wealthy, starting a business will require you to make some adjustments in how much you spend on your lifestyle.

That leads us to our final hidden truth—*there are some simple ideas you can use to prepare to start your business:*

In fact, whether you choose to start building your own business or not, putting these ideas into action can help you become more financially secure. Remember, most conflicts in marriages occur over the *lack* of money. And while money is not the key to happiness, improving your financial picture is likely to strengthen your marriage.

Tighten Your Financial Belt
This isn't as challenging as it may sound. Most households spend to the extent of their weekly, bi-weekly, or monthly income. Break your total household income into three categories—what you spend for income taxes, essential household expenses, and non-essential expenses. Here's why...

Income taxes. Too often we may forget something about income taxes. They are taxes on income. If you have an *adjusted gross income* of $100,000 in the U.S., you'll pay around $31,000 in income taxes. If you have an adjusted gross income of $0, you'll pay $0. To summarize: income means you pay taxes and no income means you pay no taxes!

Now, while no one would heartily recommend that you reduce your $100,000 income to $0 just to save on your taxes, it is still $31,000 in tax payments that you wouldn't need if you didn't have the income.

As you're probably well aware, at least in the U.S., income taxes are variable, based on your income. You need to subtract them from what you need to have each month or each year to determine what you need to survive *without* an income.

Essential household expenses. How much do you spend each month to survive? Not thrive, just *survive!*

Items that would be put into the category of essential household expenses include: food prepared and eaten at home; clothing and shoes for work and/or school; utilities; mortgage or rent payments; prescription drugs; medical expenses, both regular and unexpected; and possibly health and disability insurance (especially if you're in poor health); and property taxes.

Non-essential expenses. This is the challenging one, and probably the most important. How much of your monthly or annual income do you spend to thrive? Not just to survive, but to *thrive!*

Most of what we would purchase to fuel our *lifestyle* falls into the category of non-essentials. Entertainment, luxury items, vacations, travel, expensive clothing, high-priced cars and even eating out (regardless of whether it is at expensive restaurants or at fast food outlets) all need to be considered non-essential. Why? Because they are not essential to our survival.

Face it—a high-quality 8 oz. rib-eye steak with a baked potato, salad and dessert can cost 300 to 400 percent more if you eat it in a nice restaurant as opposed to grilling in your backyard. Checking out a movie from your local library or even renting it from a video rental store can be 10 percent of the cost of taking a family of four to the theater. It costs a lot to buy a decent new car. You may have a six-year-old family car that has thousands of miles left on it, and it is probably paid for! Why take on the extra expense of a new vehicle? If you really need another car, buy a three- or four-year-old good used one that has already been heavily depreciated!

It was true for us. We had too many financial obligations and too little ready capital to just cash it in, quit our jobs, and start our business together. We had chosen the American lifestyle of the late 20th century—live above your means. Lifestyle inflation. It's the mindset of spending more than you make because you can always make more (and pay) later—the good old installment plan!

But when we began waking up financially, and broke our household income into those three categories, (taxes, essential household expenses and non-essential household expenses) we found there were loads of places where we could cut back. Some we thought of were:

Not eating out as much as we were in the habit of doing. Eating out is expensive and usually fattening, and often not as nutritious as meals prepared at home. We do our best to keep several *quick prep* meals in the pantry and freezer so that if our day develops into one challenge after another, dinner isn't one of them.

Selecting our entertainment more carefully. In the past, if a concert, play, or special event anywhere in the area piqued our interest, we were there. We simply didn't care about the cost. There were times we walked out after two acts of a play, and there were times one of us enjoyed the concert and the other wasn't too thrilled. We had season tickets to a local professional sports team and attended less than half the games. In taking a close look at what we were doing, we realized we were wasting a *lot* of money.

Now, we are more selective in the events we attend, weighing the entertainment value for *both* of us against the price of admission. As one of the benefits, we appreciate and enjoy more fully the things we *do* attend!

Keeping better track of our charitable contributions. Almost every major fund-raising organization has a good story. It can be a challenge not to respond to every phone or mail solicitation you receive. You may think, *"I'll just send $10—how can that hurt us?"* Do that twice a month or so and then add all your regular church, synagogue, and any other contributions you make. Before long, you'll be amazed at how much money you're giving away. We had to lay down some ground rules for ourselves.

Every year we decide what five organizations, aside from our church, will receive our money. And no one else gets our charitable contributions the rest of the year. Now that our business is successful, we may give them our *time*, if we choose, but not our *money*. (Remember, your time is precious, especially as you're building your business. So be very careful how you invest it.)

And yes, it can be a challenge to say no to the Scouts and other neighborhood schoolchildren and their fundraising appeals. So we include the purchase of a few boxes of cookies and containers of popcorn in our budget then, when asked, we can say yes without breaking the bank.

In your case, you may need to limit your charitable contributions so you can invest your money in your business. Or you may need to eliminate some expensive debts like credit card balances and car payments. Again, talk to whomever is advising you on these matters, like your mentor, leader, or accountant.

We now keep a running tab of to what, when, and how much we donate every year. And we actually feel better about giving our money because we have invested the time to decide what causes are most important to us. As a result, we now feel more a part of the organizations who do receive our checks. It's a more gratifying way to be generous.

Making ourselves accountable. It is a constant endeavor to make sure our lifestyle fits our income. With self-employment, your income varies, unlike a regular paycheck job. It may seem easy to justify buying that antique hutch you've had your eye on when you finally land that big account, make a whopper sale or go to the next level in your business.

But the truth is, since you may not have had a glowing sales volume for a month or so, you probably need that money to pay your credit card bill this month. You don't want to find yourself at the end of the year asking *"Where did all our income go?"* Go *macro* and look at your total income versus your total expenditures. You may be disappointed when you realize that this is not the year to pay cash for that leather sofa you've always wanted, but you won't be putting yourself in debt either. Your time will come, as long as you keep persisting.

Essential Expenses

Grocery Shopping 101. Food is essential. One can spend $150 at the grocery store and feel okay about it because everyone has to eat. But do we need all the prepackaged, pre-prepared foods that call to us in the gourmet deli section? There are books galore on how to cut back on essential household expenses, especially groceries—coupons versus sales, warehouse versus neighborhood stores and so forth. Just be smart and savvy. That's why you're either becoming, or are, a successful businessperson. Now apply those same sound business practices as you load up your grocery cart.

Fashion "Cents." Like most women, Aprill loves to bargain shop at big fashion discount stores during their off-season sales. She'll buy a new wardrobe for next spring this fall and next fall's this spring. She may spend only $100, yet come out with three blouses, a skirt, a dress, and a pair of shoes.

On the other hand, Chuck likes to buy his ties at a specialty shop. It carries the coolest ties in town and, in our business, he needs trendy and expensive-looking ties. He's spent a lot of money on ties, but they are the ties he needs. We budget our clothing expenditures, and it really has curbed impulse bargain buys, and has given us a figure to aim for.

Take a look at your own clothing habits and how you present yourself. You may need to go on a budget, or even buy from a consignment shop, because you may have been spending too much. Keep track of your clothing expenditures for a few months and the picture will be clear.

Walking *the Plantation*.

In the warmer, longer evenings of spring and summer, we walk our *plantation*. It takes about ten minutes to stroll around the entire perimeter of our backyard if we stop to talk, point out scenery or throw a stick for the dogs. In reality and at a normal pace, it may take thirty seconds!

It's a joke we have, and it reminds us that *we have what we can comfortably afford.* And it's okay. In fact, it's more than okay—it's more than what many people have. Some don't even have a home—much less a backyard. We are grateful for what we have.

So when we think about the dream master bath we want to add or the pool or even a second house at the beach, we take a look at our income and know that we have *what we can comfortably afford.* And we feel blessed every time we pull in the driveway or emerge from the bedroom that has been converted to a second home office.

When the mortgage payment is due, it's easy to pay it. We refuse to live beyond our means, which could possibly jeopardize our business. It's just not worth it! Instant gratification with the buy-now/pay-later mentality leads to long-term pain, taking the joy out of having whatever it is you bought.

How's your *plantation*? Is it too much for you? Are you living beyond your means just to impress others? Do you realize others don't care? There are other fine *plantations* that may suit your income and your life more comfortably if you're discovering your monthly mortgage is a constant struggle to pay. Being "house poor" can get in the way of your being happy, successful businesspeople working from home.

When you walk your *plantation*, look for ways to make it well-run. Are there ways you can cut your utility bills? Are you making only necessary long-distance phone calls? Are you doing all the energy efficient things around the house that you can, such as: keeping lights off in unoccupied rooms, setting your thermostats to produce less heat or air conditioning, especially while you're sleeping, and running only full loads in the dishwasher and laundry room? These practices are good for the environment, and what you save in utility costs every month can really add up!

Some people may ask if it's okay to continue paying the neighborhood high school boy to mow their lawn, especially if their own children are too young to do it. Yes, your time is too valuable and you need to invest it in doing business activities. Just think of how many calls you could make to prospective clients or associates in the time the neighbor boy mows your lawn!

Income Taxes

Paying taxes is inexpensive rent for living in this country. And if you live outside the U.S., you could look at it the same way. Even if you don't consider it inexpensive, it's something you're unlikely to be able to change. So just accept it and take all the business deductions you're legally entitled to!

It was definitely an adjustment, though, to not have our taxes automatically deducted like they were when we got our paychecks. Depending on how and in what country you set up your business, you may pay quarterly, semi-annually, annually, or some other way. But, remember, as long as you generate an income, there will be taxes to be paid.

If you don't write your check for enough estimated taxes, or think you could get out of writing it just one time, there will be some stiff penalties. Make it a point to save for your taxes. You'll get used to it, and it'll become a habit.

Here's what we do: Out of every check you receive, you will owe taxes, so we've found it easier to take that amount out of each check (the tax offices will give you tables and percentages to use). Put it into a separate account and then deposit the rest for living expenses. You may choose to make that deposit weekly, monthly or quarterly. But you need to do it. You can't get around it.

We've had friends not pay enough only to find themselves writing a HUGE check on April 15 (U.S. Federal income tax deadline) and scrambling to cover it. We've known of others who thought maybe *they* didn't have to pay, and they lost their house, their cars, their credit ratings, and served jail time.

You don't have to like it. You can gripe and grumble and complain. You can pout over the unfairness of it all and make yourself miserable. Or you can smile that you have to pay taxes because you've got a profitable, growing business! But, whatever attitude you choose to adopt, be sure to take the correct percentage of your income and have it saved so that when you go to write the check, you'll have the money to cover it.

That First Step

Once we became committed to adjusting our lifestyle so it was more in line with where it could have been more wisely all along, something interesting happened. We couldn't wait to get our business started. Still, we had a number of options. Let's examine them. Then you'll want to discuss the best thing for you to do with your leader, mentor, or advisor.

The "Owner/Investor" Method

Description: One spouse may not be employed to begin with because the other one earns a substantial income that more than covers their expenses. Or if they both have jobs, one of them quits to devote him or herself to the new endeavor. This person takes on the role of "Owner."

The other spouse retains his or her current employment, funding not only the business start-up, but also the essential household expenses. They generate enough income to support everything. While most couples aren't in this category, some are. This person takes on the role of "Investor." Most couples don't have the luxury of this approach whereas some do. If you can financially afford this, with relative ease, you may want to consider it. Check with whomever is advising you first, though.

Pros:
- ♥ One person's focused attention on the eventual success of the business.
- ♥ Continued, reliable income from one outside source.
- ♥ Initial freedom of one partner (if they quit their job) to gain greater control of his or her life and time.
- ♥ Gradual transitional period from 100 percent employed to 100 percent self-employed.

Cons:
- ♥ Less immediate partnership and interaction.
- ♥ Some potential territoriality when the Investor eventually joins the company as Co-owner.
- ♥ Some adjustments to normal family functions (as with many new job changes).

Keys to Success:
- ♥ The spouse assuming the Owner is the chief executive officer (and many times receptionist, courier and janitor) for the company. He or she makes the decisions.
- ♥ The spouse assuming the role of Investor needs to respect the Owner's decision-making role concerning the company's direction.
- ♥ The spouse assuming the role of Investor is the principle financier of the company's operations. He or she is providing the capital. Just like with any investment, the Investor needs to question any decisions the Owner has made that the Investor sees as potentially damaging to the company, and applaud any decisions they see that further the company's growth.

♥ The spouse assuming the Owner role needs to respect any questioning of decisions the Investor chooses to ask. The Owner also needs to keep the Investor informed of the company's health, just as a Fortune 500 company does with its investors.

♥ Both the Owner and the Investor need to have goals, as well as a simple transitional plan. And they need to be in place from the beginning so when the Owner and Investor abandon their initial roles and each becomes a Co-Owner, they are ready for it.

♥ The couple needs to make it a priority to maintain an excellent non-business relationship with each other as spouses.

The Don't-Quit-Your-Day-Job Method

Description: This is the best and most realistic approach for most couples. Both maintain their full-time jobs and work together in the evenings and on weekends in the start-up of their new business.

Pros:

♥ Continued, reliable income from two outside sources to support the household and the business. With proper planning, it is virtually impossible to fall short of finances.

♥ Immediate partnership and shared objectives.

♥ More gradual transitional period from 100 percent employed to 100 percent self-employed allows the family to grow into it.

Cons:

♥ Leftover energy and concentration is given to the business venture.

♥ Time normally devoted to family activities (children's sports, pets, hobbies) is temporarily diluted.

♥ Home becomes more workplace and less sanctuary, unless most of your business is conducted with individuals and groups outside the home, such as with most direct selling businesses.

Keys to Success:
- ♥ The couple needs to form an agreement with each other to make some sacrifices of personal and leisure time for the sake of the new business.
- ♥ The couple needs to be committed to honoring and respecting the agreement.
- ♥ The couple needs to have a goal as well as a simple transitional plan in place from the beginning for when the business ceases to be a part-time, after-hours venture and becomes a full-time endeavor. This will probably include one spouse quitting (or retiring from) their job first and becoming full-time when it is financially wise to do so. It would then be followed later by the second spouse doing the same. These decisions are best made with the guidance of a mentor, leader, or other advisor.

The Part-Time Partners Method

Description: One member of the couple maintains his or her full-time job, while the other works full-time on the new business. Again, this may be feasible for those couples that can safely afford to do this because the working spouse's income is enough to support the household and the business. Both work together in the evenings and on weekends in the new business.

Pros:
- ♥ One person's focused attention on the eventual success of the business.
- ♥ Continued, reliable income from one outside source, which eliminates the fear of financial risk.
- ♥ Immediate partnership and shared objectives in new business.
- ♥ Sufficient transitional period from 100 percent employed to 100 percent self-employed.

Cons:
- ♥ Time normally devoted to family activities (children's sports, pets, hobbies) is temporarily diluted.

♥ One spouse is faced with dual-employment responsibilities while the other has the luxury of devotion to the new business.

♥ Part-time spouse can be viewed as somewhat of an outsider (perhaps by both partners).

Keys to Success:

♥ Full-time partner needs to be diligent about keeping part-time member active and involved in the business.

♥ Part-time partner needs to be committed to viewing new business as a priority.

♥ Both partners need to see new business as the future place of full-time employment for both partners for maximum results. (The actual amount of time the couple needs to devote to the business will depend somewhat on the structure of the business—including any employees and/or associates/affiliates who may help carry the load.)

Which Will You Choose?

There are certainly other options. Some work well for some people, while others work well for others. And we emphasize once again, the Don't-Quit-Your-Day-Job method. It's definitely the safest, most recommended option for the majority of couples.

For what it's worth, though, as we shared earlier, we chose the first method—Owner/Investor.

We did not have enough personal capital to fund our start-up and meet our essential household expenses without maintaining at least one job income. Plus, neither of us had the stomach for it! Neither of us wanted to potentially jeopardize our financial picture and, of course, our new business.

And that's a part of choosing how you begin. What is your gut telling you about your best chance for success? And what does your leader or mentor advise? All the books in all the world cannot give you that kind of personal guidance. Only you know, for example, how you're "wired" for risk aversion, success and failure, acceptance and rejection, exciting news and challenging news.

Are you ready to move on and live the life you want, working in partnership with your spouse? Even if you have a reluctant spouse, consider taking the step anyway. Otherwise, you'll probably regret it later, never knowing how great it could have been. So go ahead and say yes to a better future for you and your family. Running a marriage-based business will add a whole new dimension to your marriage and your life that the average working couple will sadly never understand or realize. It's a big step, no doubt. But you've taken other big steps in your life, haven't you?

Yes! You can do it. Others have and you can too. As Franklin Delano Roosevelt once said, "The only limit to our realization of tomorrow will be our doubts of today. Let us move forward with strong and active faith." So blast past any doubt you may have and go for it.

"Wherever you see a successful business, someone once made a courageous decision."

Peter Drucker

About the Authors

Aprill Jones holds a bachelor's degree in English from the State University of New York. She began her career at an HMO (health maintenance organization) in upstate New York before moving to Charlotte, NC in 1987. She was an insurance agent for 6-1/2 years until she joined the business with Chuck, her husband, and did what she had always wanted—writing and being self-employed. She is an active member at Providence Road Church of Christ where she is involved with the music ministry, is ministry leader for *Christian Women in the Workplace,* and is involved in the church's mission efforts to the City of Children in Ensenada, Mexico. Beside spending time with Chuck, she also enjoys reading, gardening, working out, loving their dogs Elmo and Stu and a cat named Big Orange, and hiking in National Parks all over the country.

Chuck Jones holds a bachelor's degree in communications from the University of Tennessee, Knoxville. He joined Garden Way Inc. (Troy, NY), a manufacturer of outdoor power equipment, in 1983. After 3-1/2 years there, he joined Washburn Direct Marketing (Charlotte, NC), rising to vice president, creative services, before leaving in 1992 to form Chuck Jones Direct Response. He is an active member of Providence Road Church of Christ serving as its Music Minister, and is involved in the church's mission efforts to the City of Children. In his spare time, he spends quality (and quantity) time with Aprill and their two dogs and one cat, enjoys all types of music, plays guitar and piano, and can occasionally be found performing at various Charlotte music venues. He loves travel, especially to the National Parks of the western U.S., and is an avid fan of the 1998 National Football Champion University of Tennessee Volunteers!

Contact Chuck and Aprill via e-mail at cjdirect@aol.com; by phone at (704)358-0302; and fax at (704)358-0309; or visit their Website at www.cjdirect.com.